This book &
Anna
CW00953876

SALES TRAINING GAMES

Sales Training Games

For Sales Managers and Trainers

GRAHAM ROBERTS-PHELPS

Gower

Published by
Gower Publishing Limited
Gower House
Croft Road
Aldershot
Hampshire GU11 3HR
England

Gower
Old Post Road
Brookfield
Vermont 05036
USA

Graham Roberts-Phelps has asserted his right under the Copyright, Designs and Patents Act 1988 to be identified as the author of this work.

British Library Cataloguing in Publication Data
Roberts-Phelps, Graham
   Sales training games : for sales managers and trainers
   1. Sales executives – Training of 2. Group games
   I. Title
   658.3'1245

ISBN 0 566 08206 3

Library of Congress Cataloging-in-Publication Data
Roberts-Phelps, Graham.
   Sales training games : for sales managers and trainers / Graham
   Roberts-Phelps.
      p. cm.
   Includes index.
   ISBN 0-566-08206-3 (hardback)
   1. Sales personnel—Training of. 2. Selling—Problems, exercises,
   etc. I. Title.
   HF5439.8.R63   1999
   658.3'1245—dc21   99–40395
                                                                          CIP

Typeset in 11 point Palatino by Bournemouth Colour Press, Parkstone and printed in Great Britain by MPG Books Ltd, Bodmin.

Contents

Summary of games

Ice-breakers and energizers

Subject breakers

Models and methods

value and closing percentage, and practise applying it to measure their own sales performance.

Quizzes and questionnaires

Group energizers

Role plays, practice sessions and case studies

their back' – no questions or benefits allowed in the exchange!

Skill boosters

A collection of trigger questions, tasks and ideas to liven up any training or coaching session.

1

Introduction

About this manual

These activities have been created and used extensively in the training of sales skills. Relevant to all types of industry and successful with personnel of any age, experience and background, they are designed with the following characteristics in mind.

Easy to run

Simple to follow, step-by-step instructions mean that a minimum of preparation and experience is required. The time saved can then be devoted to either enhancing the basic activity or creating company-specific material.

Complete

Each activity comes with everything necessary – including handouts.

Generic

Whether you are a manufacturer or a service provider, private or public sector, industrial or retail, the activities and exercises are focused on generic sales knowledge and skills – skills that are completely transferable across all organizations and situations. Most use an 'open content' approach, which means that participants use their own examples and experiences as the main subject, making the exercises automatically and completely

1

relevant. (They are, of course, easy to customize should you wish to do so.)

Varied

The activities range from 15-minute ice-breakers to 90-minute role plays and include quizzes, games, questionnaires, problem-solving activities and discussions. This means that the training can be kept varied and interesting, and topics approached from several different angles.

How to use this manual

Each activity is detailed in a clear set of instructions for the trainer, with information contained under the following headings.

Summary and objectives

These give a short summary of the aims of the activity. In many of the activities it is recommended that you share the objectives with the participants as it will help them to focus when completing the activity.

Materials

These are quick checklists of what you will need to run the activity. In most cases a standard flip chart and the handouts provided are all that are required.

Timing

Estimated times are based on a group size of 8–10 participants. Less or more time may be needed if the group is smaller or larger than this. The estimates are generous, as exercises are more likely to over run than under run. This also allows for trainers or managers to expand the introduction or exercise summary sessions with their own material or examples.

Handouts

These follow the trainer's notes, contain instructions to the participants on how to perform the task or activity, and often provide a structured format or worksheet. The benefit of using the handouts provided is that the communication is often much clearer, as it gives participants a reference during the exercise.

Procedure

This section details the training instructions and explains how to introduce, run and conclude each activity. These instructions are kept deliberately brief. This is of great benefit when referring to the notes whilst running the course, as the information you need can be easily found, read and relayed to the group.

Instructions have been phrased in a general way, and, where possible, avoid giving the actual words to be used (as very few trainers will use them, choosing instead to use their own words).

Actions

When you are required to distribute a handout, the instructions are set in bold type to stand out from the main text. Although this may repeat an instruction contained in the main paragraph, it is an aid to quick reference when you are running the exercise.

Commentary

These sections add extra information, ideas and tips when needed.

The main formats of games and activities

Individual working

When participants are required to work on their own, perhaps completing a questionnaire or worksheet, it allows for a degree of self-reflection and is an excellent contrast to the role play and group work. Many people are happy working in this way, indeed it follows the pattern of learning established at school.

Pairs

Based on the principle that 'two heads are better that one', this format needs participants to work in pairs, working through a problem, questionnaire or worksheet jointly.

It is useful to pair people carefully, balancing personalities and experience. Make sure that both are contributing and making notes. On longer courses, it is a good idea to change these pairs occasionally. If the numbers of participants are odd, one group can be stretched to three.

Small groups

Small groups of 3–8 people are most suitable for working on a problem, issue or discussion, as well as in free-format ideas sessions.

The size of your main group will of course determine how small you can divide the groups, but from general observation it is difficult to circulate between or monitor more than about four groups.

Main group discussion

The whole group (of eight or more people) might run a general discussion or activity.

Role plays

The series of role plays included in the book can be used in isolation or as on-going exercises during the training course. There is one for each major part of the sales cycle, or sales skill. If you are using an extended series of role plays, it is best if participants use the same customer example throughout. In this way, continuity can be maintained and the sales progressed stage by stage.

These role-play customers can be based on real customers taken from the salesperson's existing accounts. Alternatively, you may wish to create your own sample case studies. The observation checklist and action plans included here can be used for all the role plays.

Observer's checklist

When running role plays, some guidance is normally required to help participants act as 'observers', and offer constructive feedback. Here are some questions that might help observers assess role-play situations.

- What worked well? Be specific.
- What particularly impressed you?
- What do you think could be improved?
- What could be done differently next time?
- What did you learn?

- What did you notice about non-verbal behaviour? Consider: body language and physiology; seating arrangements, use of props, notes, handouts, etc.; eye contact, physical contact and proximity.
- Did the salespersons achieve their objectives? Were these stated or apparent?
- How would you rate the overall role play, on a scale of one to ten?

Role-play observation sheet

Name:

Skill	Check	Example
Gained rapport		
Introduction		
Used fact-finding questions		
Tested understanding		
Summarized		
Empathized		
Stayed calm		
Controlled conversation		
Explained reasons		
Mentioned benefits		
Avoided negatives		
Avoided jargon		
Being defensive		
Talking over		
Handling disagreement		

Were objectives met?
What worked well?
What particularly impressed you?
What could be improved?
What else did you learn or notice?

Five tips to get the best out of this manual

1. Use the exercises with confidence

All the activities and games in this manual have been developed and used in professional training courses and seminars, and are all proven to be effective on different types of course and with a variety of participants.

2. Be flexible

Because of the 'open content' style, the activities are suitable for most types of organizations and training courses. This approach also makes them easy to adapt to your needs.

You might want to experiment and develop your own variations of these activities and games, for example by adding in new elements or lengthening particular segments. You will also find that because of the 'open-content' nature of the activities they will vary slightly in execution, with different groups having different reactions and results.

3. Structure your training

By mixing at least three different formats (working in small groups/pairs, as individuals and in the group as a whole) to cover the same points, you can greatly increase learning retention and effectiveness. People will have different preferences and gain more from changing these formats during a course.

4. Make notes and adapt

Don't be afraid to customize or edit these activities to suit your own style of training better as you gain experience in running them. Make notes in the margin whilst preparing the course or during it in order to remember the points for next time.

5. Train, don't talk

Most of the trainer's time is spent not telling people what to do, rather trying to get them to **do** what they already **know**. These activities and games are designed to help people learn. If you find yourself talking rather less than you might do normally, don't worry about it!

An overview of the activities and exercises

Ice-breakers and energizers

These activities will serve to raise the energy level in a group and encourage people to work together in pairs or groups in a lively and fun manner.

Subject breakers

These activities are designed to be used at the beginning of a training course, session or meeting. They serve to introduce a subject, topic or issue. Most will get people working together and create a 'buzz' in the room.

Models and methods

This collection of training exercises applies proven sales models to the participants' own situations, with the aim of improving skills and knowledge levels.

Quizzes

A collection of different types of generic quizzes and questionnaires.

Group energizers

More games and activities to get participants working together in groups.

Problem-solving and planning

A series of activities to facilitate creative thinking around and analysis of current working practises and standards.

Role plays, practice sessions and case studies

A collection of generic role-play activities and practice sessions.

Skill boosters

A collection of handouts giving short tasks, trigger questions and discussion topics suitable as meeting activities or as part of a larger training module.

2

Ice-breakers and energizers

Purpose   Ice-breakers and energizers can be used to start a session, mark a change of topics or pace, or offer a lively interlude.

Process   The exercises vary in their format and duration, although all require little preparation and most last only a few minutes.

Activities   Gift of the gab
Personal introductions with a twist
Three-letter words
Acronym quiz
Human bingo
Jargon quiz
Three things in common
Cricket practice
Ten questions about you
Sales graffiti
Euroland quiz

Gift of the Gab

Summary   Participants try to communicate a word or phrase to their team members without actually using that word or phrase. (A game inspired by 'articulate' – a derivative of charades.)

Objectives   ice-breaking
energizing
encouraging quick thinking and expression

Materials   Handout provided

Timing   5 minutes

Procedure   1. Form the group into two teams. Alternatively, with a group of more than 12, form them into four teams of 3–5 people. Team A versus team B, and team C versus team D.
2. Ask each team to select a 'talker'.
3. Distribute the handout to the talkers and agree who will go first. The talker in the nominated team has one minute to describe as many words as possible to their team mates, without mentioning the 'target' word directly. (If they do, they are 'out'.) Once the correct definition is shouted out, they can continue on to the next word. They can pass on any words if they wish. Each correctly identified word or phrase scores two points.

Run the rounds, one team at a time, keeping scores on a flip-chart or board

4. After three rounds per team, read out the scores, and award small prizes, for example chocolate bars, to the winners.

Gift of the Gab

1. Choose a column, either 1, 2 or 3.
2. Describe the phrase, place, object or person to your team without actually mentioning the words directly. Each round is played for one minute and the objective is for your team to guess as many as possible.
3. You may pass and return to a word at any time.
4. Once your team has guessed a word, move on to the next, until the one minute is up.

1. Activity	2. People	3. Things
Falling asleep	David Bowie	The Eiffel Tower
Travelling on a train	Margaret Thatcher	Jelly
	Einstein	A refrigerator
Eating an Indian meal	Guy Fawkes	A sticking plaster
	Mickey Mouse	Toothpaste
Riding a bike	Richard Branson	Spot cream
Going to the dentist	Clint Eastwood	Lager
Typing on a computer	Tony Blair	A key ring
	Darth Vader	Frying pan
Shaking hands	The Spice Girls	A screw driver
Watching television	Lynford Christie	Fork lift truck
Reading a book	Henry VIII	Cricket box
Getting dressed	Mick Jagger	
Having an idea	Salman Rushdie	
Kissing	President Yeltsin	

Personal introductions with a twist

Summary   Participants introduce themselves in a novel and humorous way.

Objectives   ice-breaking
confidence building
energizing

Materials   Post-it notes or index cards

Timing   5 minutes preparation, plus 2 minutes per participant

Procedure   1.   Write the following introduction styles on post-it notes or index cards and give one to each participant. Repeat items if necessary – some participants will have duplicate cards.

- TV game show host
- Evangelical preacher
- TV newsreader
- Commercial radio DJ
- Rather stuffy, old, ex-Major
- Football commentator
- Nine-year-old child
- Film star of your choice
- Cartoon character of your choice
- Used car salesperson

2.   Ask each person to prepare a short personal introduction, i.e. his or her current job, previous jobs, personal interests, and so on, to be presented in the style written on the card.

Three-letter words

Summary   A version of the traditional word game, in which participants work in pairs against the clock to create as many two-letter and three-letter (or more) words out of a longer, sales-related word.

Objectives   session starter or break between sessions

Materials   Handouts provided (word quiz and word challenge)

Timing   5 minutes

Procedure   1.   Distribute either of the handouts. Ask participants to work in pairs and generate as many new words as they can from the original word.
2.   After three minutes, ask participants to read out their answers. Award small prizes, such as chocolate bars, to the winners.

Word quiz

Working in pairs take three minutes to see how many three-letter words you can make from the following word.

PERSUASION

Word challenge

Working in pairs take three minutes to see how many three-letter words you can make from the following word.

CUSTOMERS

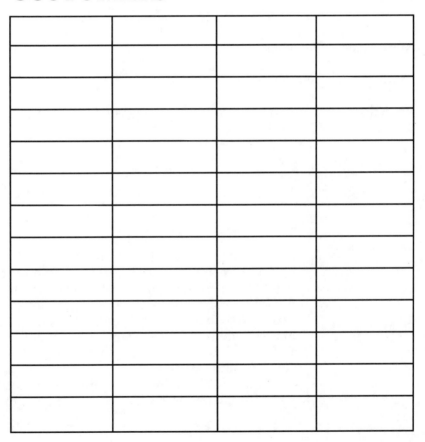

Acronym quiz

Summary   A competitive game in which teams try to identify the correct meaning of abbreviations and acronyms.

Objectives energizer
                teamwork

Materials   Flip chart

Timing   10 minutes

Procedure
1. Write the following suggested acronyms on a flip chart, adding any or your own.

IBM	ASAP	FOB
SWOT	RSVP	BMW
AEG	RAM	ROM
WYSIWYG	VAT	FOC
E&OE		

2. Divide the group into two or more teams.
3. Ask each member of each team to come up one at a time, point to an acronym on the list and shout what it stands for. Award two points for right answer, one for an answer that is close. Offer unanswered items to the other team. For more fun, include some spoof items, such as IDK (I don't know) and NAC (not a clue). You could also include terms from your training course.
4. Continue until all the acronyms are correctly identified. Award small prizes, such as chocolate bars, to the winners.

Human bingo

Summary   Participants circulate with a 'Bingo' card listing personal attributes. By talking to everyone in the room, the objective is to achieve a 'full house', by matching the attributes to the people on the course.

Objectives   ice-breaking
energizing

Materials   Handout provided

Timing   10–15 minutes

Procedure   1.   Distribute the handout provided or your own version.
2.   Ask participants to circulate around the room as quickly as they can, identifying and writing the name of the appropriate person in each box.
3.   Keep going until most people have got a 'full house'.

Commentary   This activity is a good way to start a session, particularly for a larger meeting or conference or where people may know each other and traditional ice-breakers are not really relevant. It can also be good in building teams of people and encouraging them to share information about each other in an informal, light-hearted and non-threatening manner.

You might want to include one or two red herrings that do not 'belong' to anybody just to encourage people to think carefully.

This is a good exercise to introduce the subject of stereotyping.

Human bingo

Circulate around the room and find the name of at least one person for each box. Write their name in the space provided.

Is over 6 feet tall	Speaks two languages	Has a tattoo
_____	_____	_____
Is bald (or nearly)	Drives a red car	Has run a marathon
_____	_____	_____
Can juggle or do a magic trick	Has a famous friend or relative	Plays a musical instrument regularly
_____	_____	_____

Jargon quiz

Summary   Participants work in pairs to generate multiple definitions for phrases of sales-related jargon.

Objectives warning of the dangers of jargon

Materials   Handout provided

Timing   10–15 minutes

Procedure   1. Distribute the handout and ask participants to work in pairs to generate as many definitions as they can for each of the phrases listed.
2. After 7–10 minutes, ask participants to read out their answers. Award small prizes, such as chocolate bars, to the winners.

You might choose your own terms or jargon from the course you are running.

Jargon quiz

Work in pairs and review the list of the terms below and see against how many you can write definitions.

Term	Definition or full meaning
Open question	
Closed question	
Test close	
Off the page offer	
Cold call	
Referral	
Cross sell	
S.P.I.F.	
Net profit	
Gross profit	
Buyer's remorse	
The 4 Ps	
Customer churn	

Three things in common

Summary   Participants introduce themselves to someone they have not met before and then try to find three things they have in common.

Objectives   rapport-building

Materials   Flip chart

Timing   15 minutes, plus discussion

Procedure
1. Ask participants to circulate around the room and introduce themselves to another participant, ideally someone they have not met before, and find three things that they have in common.
2. After 10 minutes, participants should return to their seats. Ask each participant, in turn, to say what they were able to identify in common with the other person. In a larger group, do this for 10 participants, or until themes begin to repeat themselves.
3. If anybody has had a real problem in finding things in common, you could suggest that the three things in common, might be:

   - on the course together,
   - both in sales,
   - both work for the same company, live in the same area.

4. Run a short group discussion around the following themes, making a note of key points that arise on a flip chart.

   - How easy was it to find things in common?
   - What type of questions did you ask?
   - Is the exercise effective in building rapport and empathy?

21

- How do you feel towards people who only 10 minutes ago were (perhaps) total strangers?
- What questions would you ask if you did the exercise again?

This exercise is particularly good with large groups.

Highlight in the discussion that one of the fastest ways of building trust and rapport is to demonstrate to people that 'you are like them'. This is achieved by finding things that you can both associate with, relate to or have in common. This is also a skill of good mass-communicators, who are able to say things that the whole audience may have in common or with which they agree.

Cricket practice

Summary
Using a soft ball to pick out participants, the trainer challenges them to shout out a feature and then a benefit of a nominated product or service.

Objectives
warm up or summary
testing knowledge and understanding

Materials
Soft ball

Timing
10–15 minutes

Procedure
1. Explain that you will throw a soft ball to someone, which they must then catch, and then immediately think of a feature of the nominated product or service and throw the ball back to **you** as they say it. You will then throw it to another participant who must catch it and quickly shout a benefit associated with that particular feature. Any participant who takes more than 10 seconds to answer is 'timed out' and has to throw the ball back.
    So, as you throw the ball, you will be shouting alternately 'feature' and then 'benefit'.
2. Nominate a product or service.
3. Start the exercise.
4. Repeat until most participants have had at least two or three catches.

You can make it more difficult by ensuring a fast pace, and, of course, it becomes more difficult as the more obvious features and benefits are used up.

Ten questions about you

Summary   Ten questions to enable participants to reflect on their beliefs, perceptions, strengths and weaknesses.

Objectives   self-assessment
self-awareness

Materials   Handout provided, flip chart

Timing   10–15 minutes, plus discussion

Procedure   1. Introduce the exercise with the objective of considering personal strengths and weaknesses objectively.
2. Distribute the handout provided to participants and ask them to work through the ten questions carefully and thoughtfully, taking time to think through each one. Remind participants that there are no right or wrong answers, rather the answers will lead them to greater self-knowledge and self-improvement. Assure them that the papers will not be reviewed or 'marked' by anybody but themselves, unless they choose otherwise.

Distribute the handout and allow 10–15 minutes.

3. Although group review may be difficult because of the personal nature of the questions, a structured discussion around key questions may be useful to prompt contributions.

   • Which questions were the most difficult to answer?
   • Are there any answers that surprised you?
   • Which questions do you feel were the most useful?

This is a good exercise to change pace in a training environment. After considerable group or syndicate work, it will allow participants to work quietly on their own, reflecting on their strengths and weaknesses.

Ten questions about you

Work carefully and thoughtfully through these questions, taking time to think through any that you are unsure of. There are no right or wrong answers, instead your answers will lead you to greater self-knowledge and self-improvement. Make notes on a separate sheet of paper.

Question

1. If you could have any position or job you wanted, what would you do?
2. What qualities do you feel you have that are most valuable to the company?
3. What qualities do you have that you feel are currently under-used?
4. What do you feel has been the greatest accomplishment in your life?
5. What has been your greatest disappointment?
6. What have you done in the past year to improve yourself?
7. What factors in your past have contributed most to your own development?
8. Who do you consider to be the most successful person you have ever met? Why?
9. What really motivates you?
10. What really de-motivates you?

Sales graffiti

Summary   Participants think up and write 'sales graffiti' on flip chart pages posted around the room.

Objectives   ice-breaking
energizing

Materials   Flip chart pages

Timing   15–20 minutes

Procedure
1. Introduce the exercise by asking participants when they last saw graffiti on a wall. Continue by stating that the trouble with most graffiti is that it is too boring and unimaginative.
2. Explain that you are going to create your own graffiti to brighten up the training room, but that this graffiti should be inspirational, motivating and remind people of key sales techniques.
3. Divide participants into groups of 2–3 and hand them several sheets of flip chart paper each. Ask participants to write some 'sales graffiti' on the paper, which you will then pin around the wall. (You could alternatively cover a wall with flip chart paper and ask participants to write directly on the wall, allocating a section to each group.)

Allow 10–15 minutes.

4. Next pin the flip chart pages around the room and refer to them as necessary to draw attention to key points during the training course. You could use the following list of sample graffiti phrases.

    ● Smile while you dial.
    ● People buy with emotion and justify with fact.

- Attitudes are contagious – is yours worth catching?
- The customer is not always right, but they are always the customer.
- Customers make pay-days possible, sales people make customers possible.
- Don't just sit there, **sell** something.
- Sales people do it persistently.
- I'd rather be selling.
- If you don't know why I love selling, then you wouldn't understand.
- You never know which phone call will be the next order.
- You're already dealing with your best customer.
- Telling is not selling.
- Can't is a four letter word.
- Sell products that don't come back to people who do.
- The person who talks the most dominates the conversation, the person who asks the most questions, controls it.
- Persistence only works when nothing else does.
- Nobody plans to fail – they just fail to plan.
- Nobody likes to be sold, but everybody likes to buy.
- Selling is the closest you can get to another human being, with your clothes on!
- Clients buy people, not products.

Euroland quiz

Summary   A competitive quiz to name the European currencies.

Objectives   team work
                 energizing

Materials   Handout provided

Timing   10–15 minutes

Procedure
1. Introduce the exercise by mentioning how the introduction of the Euro currency, whilst not welcomed by everybody, should make it simpler when doing business or travelling in Europe.
2. Distribute the handout and ask participants to work in pairs and find the existing currency of each country.
3. After 10 minutes, ask the participants to read out their answers. Award small prizes, such as chocolate bars, to the winners (namely, the pair with the most correct answers).

Euroland quiz

Country	Currency
Austria	Schilling
Belgium	
Bulgaria	
Cyprus	
Czech Republic	
Denmark	
Finland	
France	
Germany	
Greece	
Hungary	
Iceland	
Italy	
Luxembourg	
Malta	
Monaco	
Netherlands	
Norway	
Poland	
Portugal	

cont'd

Country	Currency
Romania	
Soviet Republic	
Spain	
Sweden	
Turkey	
UK	

3

Subject breakers

Purpose   'Subject breakers' are designed to literally introduce or 'break-in'
a topic. They are designed to help you to move quickly and
smoothly into an interactive and participative exercise with only
a brief introduction.

Process   Participants work in pairs or small groups to work on a
discussion exercise. They then write their answers on flip chart
and present back. A general discussion can then be run as
appropriate.

Activities   Helping buyers to buy
Sales presentation – 'do's and 'don't's
Customer-focused selling
Cold-calling blues!
The sales factory
Who or what won the sale?
Nothing happens until someone sells something

Helping buyers to buy

Summary   An exercise in empathy in which participants explore selling from the customer's perspective, by brainstorming how they would like to be sold to. It highlights the importance of adopting professional and low-pressure sales techniques that help people to buy in the way with which they are most comfortable.

Objectives   consideration of the customer's viewpoint

Materials   Handout provided, flip chart

Timing   15 minutes, plus discussion

Procedure
1. Explain that participants will be asked to look at selling from the buyer's perspective, and consider how they might like to be sold to.
2. Divide participants into pairs or small groups and distribute the handout provided. Explain that participants should work on the questions for 15 minutes, after which time they will be invited to share their ideas in a general discussion.

Distribute the handout and allow about 15 minutes (this could be extended if desired).

3. When most people have finished, review each question in turn, discussing them fully before moving on. Make sure that all the groups contribute, and summarize key points on flip chart. You can prompt discussion with the following questions.

    ● Do you ever consider how you might **look** or appear to a customer?
    ● Would you buy from you?
    ● How can we project the qualities that customers expect?

- If these are the things customers would like us to do ... why don't we, or other salespeople, do them now?
- How does seeing things from the customer's viewpoint change the image we have of ourselves?

Helping buyers to buy

Imagine that you are now the buyer of your products and services. Describe how you would like to be **sold** to, in other words how you would want a salesperson to act and treat you. Make notes on a separate sheet of paper. Be ready to share your ideas with the rest of the group at the end of the exercise.

If you were a customer ...

1. How would you like the salesperson to make 'first contact'?
2. What would you like your salesperson to look like?
3. What problems do you face in trying to make a correct buying decision for this type of product or service?
4. Describe in detail the approach that you would require from an ideal salesperson, and what would impress you and encourage you to purchase.
5. What would put you off making a decision with a particular salesperson or company?
6. What questions would you like the salesperson to ask you?
7. What information would you need from the salesperson, or like them to offer you in order to make a confident buying decision?
8. What sort of things could the salesperson do or say to impress you?
9. What sort of things could the salesperson do or say that would not impress you?
10. Relative to other considerations, how important is price? What might persuade you to pay slightly more than you anticipated for something?

Sales presentation – 'do's and 'don't's

Summary   Working in small groups, participants brainstorm and then present the key 'do's and 'don't's of successful selling.

Objectives   (re)discovery of knowledge of key skills

Materials   Handouts provided, flip chart

Timing   20 minutes, plus discussion

Procedure

1. Introduce this exercise by stating that it will help participants to (re)discover their own knowledge of key skills and behaviours when presenting features, benefits and solutions in a sales call.
2. Divide the whole group into smaller groups of two or three people and distribute the handout to each of the groups.
3. Ask the groups to complete their own 'do's and 'don't's. Stress the importance of identifying clear, specific actions and behaviours. If participants are not sure of what the answers should be, ask them to apply some common sense; that is, after all, 90 per cent of selling skills.

Distribute the handout and allow 10–15 minutes.

4. After 10–15 minutes, or when everybody has finished, ask each group to present their list of of 'do's and 'don't's using a flip chart.
5. At the end of each presentation ask if any participants have any other questions. Ask the participants to make a note of key points from others. You can review key points with a group discussion.

It may be useful to prepare your own list of 'do's and 'don't's when running the exercise for the first time.

Sales presentation – 'do's and 'don't's

What advice would you give to somebody (the rest of the group) about what you should and should not do; in other words the key skills, when presenting features, benefits and solutions in a sales call.

'Do's	'Don't's

Customer-focused selling

Summary   Working in small groups, participants brainstorm solutions to trigger questions about effective closing.

Objectives   generating and developing ideas
discussion of key closing techniques
reinforcing learning points
self-analysis

Materials   Flip chart

Timing   30 minutes, plus discussion

Procedure
1. Introduce the exercise by highlighting its objectives. Explain that it is a very good way of accessing and sharing the knowledge, ideas and expertise of more experienced or successful salespeople with everyone in the group.
2. Write the following trigger questions on the flip chart, or read them out to the group and ask them to write them down.

    ● What are some of reasons why salespeople don't ask for the order or attempt to close the sale?
    ● How can you close any sale in a way that makes customers feel that they have 'bought' rather than been 'sold'?

3. Divide participants into groups of 4–8 and ideally use different rooms for their discussions. Allow at least 20 minutes.

Divide into groups and allow 20 minutes to work.

4. Set participants the task of summarizing the main points and considering the consequences to themselves as salespeople. Allow a further five minutes.

5. Ask each group to elect a spokesperson who can present their main conclusions and allow each group about 10 minutes, with extra time for discussion as appropriate. You could use the following reasons for not closing the sale.

    ● Not knowing how.
    ● Not knowing when; unable to recognize buying signals.
    ● To friendly – don't want to upset the customer.
    ● Too nice, as above.
    ● Rushing.
    ● Fear of failure.
    ● Fear of rejection.

Cold-calling blues!

Summary   An exercise for small groups to explore the reasons for – and solutions to – salespeople's 'call reluctance'. In other words why people avoid, or are at least 'reluctant' to make prospecting or sales calls – especially cold-calls.

Objectives   introduction to selling by telephone
self-analysis

Materials   Handouts provided, flip chart

Timing   30–40 minutes

Procedure   1. Ask participants if they have ever experienced 'call reluctance' when selling or prospecting by telephone. It is often disguised as 'having' to write a letter or doing something else – anything to avoid getting back on the phone.
      Explain that on a statistical basis every call counts in making sales – even the 'unsuccessful' ones (selling is still a 'numbers game'). So why is it that nearly all of us from time to time are 'reluctant' to make prospecting calls?
2. Divide the group into pairs. Distribute the first handout provided and ask the pairs to spend 15 minutes discussing the points on the handout.

Distribute the first handout and allow 15 minutes.

3. After 15 minutes, or when most people have finished, ask each pair in turn to summarize their responses to each question. Convert these into a general group discussion by writing them on a flip chart and developing themes as appropriate.

You may find the following points useful to prompt the discussion. Reasons why people don't like to make calls:

- Fear/anxiety
- Don't know how/lack of skill
- Not organized/not enough time
- Not motivated/no clear goals or direction
- Do not like using the phone
- Not successful at this method
- Intimidated by senior people/difficult 'gate-keepers'

Things to improve or cure 'cold-calling blues':

- Skills in telephone techniques
- Lists to work from
- Getting past assistants and secretaries
- Call-tracking system
- Time planning/personal organization
- Daily/weekly cold-call goals and sessions
- Make it more fun, remove anxiety
- Get motivated (how and by whom?)

4. Distribute the second handout and work through it, highlighting the key points, and adding any points that were missed during initial discussions.
5. Form participants back into the pairs and ask each to pick one or two of the most important reasons for call reluctance and identify three solutions for each.
6. After 5–10 minutes, re-form the main group and ask each pair in turn to present their solutions and list them on the flip chart.

1. Cold-calling blues!

Take time to reflect on these questions, making some notes. Be ready to contribute these to the group discussion which will follow.

1. On a statistical basis every call counts in making sales – even the 'unsuccessful' ones (selling is still a 'numbers game'). So why is it that nearly all of us from time to time are 'reluctant' to make calls, and what are the reasons that stop us making more prospecting calls?

   _____

   _____

   _____

   _____

   _____

2. What could we do, or what would have to happen, for us to make more calls and overcome our 'call reluctance'?

   _____

   _____

   _____

   _____

   _____

2. Cold-calling blues!

1. Poor organization

- Energy diverted into non-critical areas, such as paperwork
- Too much preparation and planning; not enough action
- Over-complicated process – too much jargon, and so on
- No system for tracking and following up on calls

2. Low self-esteem

- Does not relate sales success to the spade work of prospecting
- Takes himself or herself (or cold-calling) too seriously
- Considers telephone prospecting 'unprofessional' or belittling
- Poor self-image or does not see himself or herself as a salesperson
- Hesitation due to seniority or manner of person
- Gets too emotionally involved – takes rejection personally
- Lack of support from others to aid self-motivation

3. Low skill level

- Prefers face-to-face meetings and contacts
- Lack of skill in using telephone
- Difficulty in getting through to contacts
- Lack of lists or contacts
- Unaware of potential benefits/conversion ratios

4. Negative attitude

- Negative attitude, such as 'Nobody's interested …'
- Uncomfortable as feels this is intrusive
- Easily distracted from telephone work
- Excusitis – always an excuse, never a reason

The sales factory

Summary   Using the analogy of a manufacturing process, participants work to record the complete sales process and the key stages within it.

Objectives   identification of a structured approach to sales

Materials   Handouts provided, flip chart

Timing   30 minutes

Procedure
1. Introduce the exercise by likening a sale, or indeed the whole sales process, to that of a factory or production line. The raw, unrefined, materials come in one end, are put through a series of carefully managed processes and finished goods are produced at the other end.
2. Distribute the handout provided and ask participants to work in groups of 2–3.

Distribute handout 1 and allow 15 minutes.

3. After 15 minutes, ask the participants to share their conclusions and summarize the various steps on a flip chart.
4. Review the following list or use a list developed by yourself or a previous group and ask for comments on how it relates to the sales process or framework that they have just defined.

i. Positioning
Marketing, prospecting, referrals, PR

ii. Rapport building
Greeting and initial qualification; hook (create interest/gain attention); state purpose or reason for call/appointment; close for next stage of sale; handle put-downs

iii. Need identification and creation

Further qualification – money, authority, need, willingness, time scales, and so forth; gather information – business type, structure, size, style; identify any problems or areas for improvements; identify current and future plans and projects; assess and develop desire or willingness to change

iv. Building desire, establishing proof

Summary of needs; offer solution (benefits); cost justify (logic); present final solution and create enthusiasm and urgency

v. Decision, commitment and action

Handle questions; handle and answer objections; gain commitment – close the sale; avoid discounts; sell up

vi. Internal processing

Order fulfilment; sales reporting; market information

vii. Follow-through

Post-sales follow-through (internal); call back and check all is well; set future plans; obtain referrals; increase the rate of growth (back to (ii))

You might use the following questions to prompt the discussion

- Is this model true for the majority of sales?
- What might vary from customer to customer or sale to sale?
- Would you tell the customer the steps that you are going to take them through?
- What are the benefits to you (the salesperson) of applying a model like this to your sales approach?
- What are the benefits to the customer?
- When wouldn't you want to use this approach?
- Are there any variations or alterations that you could make to improve it even further?
- How can you remind yourself of this model on a daily basis?

5. Close the session by stressing the importance of completing the sales sequence systematically and completely for each sales situation. Just in the same way that automated

production techniques have revolutionized industry, so a carefully planned and followed sales 'process' can help to make more productive salespeople.

The sales factory

A sale, or indeed the whole sales process, can be likened to that of a factory or production line. The raw, unrefined, materials come in one end, are put through a series of carefully managed processes and finished goods are produced at the other end.

Working in groups of two or three, take time to define some or all of the stages that your customer must pass through in order for a sale to be successful.

You might like to start with when you first contact the customer, or prospective customer, and finish with a call for a referral a few weeks after the sale has been completed.

_____

_____

_____

_____

_____

_____

Who or what won the sale?

Summary   A sales 'whodunit' in which participants identify the factors behind a successful sale and are encouraged to learn from success.

Objectives   focusing on strengths and how to build on them

Materials   Handout provided, flip chart

Timing   30–40 minutes, plus discussion

Procedure
1. Introduce the exercise as a sort of sales 'whodunit'. Using their skills of detection and analysis, the participants will try and discover why a particular sale was won, and what lessons can be learnt by the example.
2. Distribute the handout provided and ask participants to work in pairs, working through the questions as thoroughly as possible. Explain that each person in the pair should take 15 minutes.

Distribute the handout and allow 30 minutes.

3. After 30 minutes, ask the group to reassemble and ask each participant to review his or her example and conclusions, going through each of the four questions in turn.
4. Develop group discussion by asking the participants to consider the following questions, and make a note of any points on the flip chart.

   ● What lessons or key points can be learned?
   ● How easy was it to analyse the sale in this way?

It is as valuable to focus on elements and actions that contributed to a successful sale as it is to analyse occasions when sales are lost. Be aware of the 'because I'm such a good salesperson' syndrome and concentrate the groups on the specifics of the situations they are describing.

Who or what won the sale?

The purpose of this exercise is to help identify areas for self-development and improvement.

Take a moment to select a recent (or current) sale that you have won or is going very well, or a sales call that went well.

Customer: _____

Brief details:

_____

_____

_____

On a separate sheet of paper, and working in a small group, consider the following questions. Be prepared to present your analysis to the group.

1. What reasons did the customer give for going ahead with you?
2. What reasons do you believe, honestly, contributed to the call being successful or the customer buying? List all the factors you think apply, giving details and reasons where appropriate.
3. If you could wave a magic wand and start the sale over again, what would you do differently? Be as specific and as detailed as you can.
4. What lessons can you learn from this sale that can help you in future sales?

Nothing happens until someone sells something

Summary   An exercise in which non-specialist sales staff (customer service, service engineers and so forth) can challenge their negative perceptions of selling.

Objectives   building a positive self image

Materials   Handouts provided, flip chart

Timing   30 minutes

Procedure

1. Introduce the exercise by asking participants what is the typical reaction that people have towards salespeople. This will probably draw a negative response for example 'pushy', 'unreliable' or 'fast-talking'. Explain that during this exercise you will enable people to challenge this traditional and unflattering view of sales and selling.
2. Write on the flip chart: 'Nothing happens until someone sells something.' Ask participants what they think it means and if they agree with it.

Explain that in this exercise you are going to focus on the importance of selling in the overall scheme of things, and how reminding ourselves of this can help us have a positive self-image, and see ourselves as sales professionals, adding real value and worth through our efforts and achievements.

3. Distribute the handouts and ask the participants to complete them in pairs.

Distribute the handouts and allow 15–20 minutes.

53

4. After 15–20 minutes reassemble the group and review the questions one at a time, gathering responses, encouraging discussion and making notes on the flip chart as required. You might prompt discussion with the following questions.

- Could business survive without salespeople of one sort or another?
- Would the orders that you create, happen if you didn't make the initial contacts and follow them through?
- How does selling increase the customer's satisfaction and add value to the products and services?
- Are sales-led organizations developing faster and more exciting organizations?

It is important that you have prepared sample answers for the questions, based on the responses you would ideally like participants to give. (Note: The answer to question 1 on the handout is statistically (for the UK) one salesperson for every 40 employees.)

You may find that some participants answer the questions humorously. These responses may still be used to make a point if you look behind the humour. A jokey response may mean these salespeople are not used to taking themselves too seriously, which is a good survival mechanism in selling.

The net result of the exercise is that you want salespeople to **be proud** to be salespeople and realize that their success creates jobs, profits, and value for their customers.

This exercise is ideal for new salespeople or for those who are perhaps having to sell as part of a more diverse role (for example, service engineers and customer service staff) and are perhaps a little doubtful about selling.

Positive self-image

It is useful to remind yourself of how important selling is to your company and the economy as a whole. This process will highlight the positive role you play as a salesperson. Self-esteem is an important ingredient for successful selling. Take time to reflect on and answer the following questions.

1. What is the ratio of salespeople to employees in your company? (How many people are employed per salesperson?)	
2. List three major benefits that your customer gains by buying from you.	1. 2. 3.
3. List three major benefits that your company gains when you are successful as a sales professional.	1. 2. 3.
4. List three major benefits that you gain when you are successful as a sales professional.	1. 2. 3.

cont'd

Reproduced from *Sales Training Games*, Graham Roberts-Phelps, Gower, Aldershot 55

5. How do you add value to a product or service by the **way** that you sell something? (Give examples where possible.)	
6. How much business would your company do if it didn't have any salespeople?	
7. How would you like a customer to describe you?	
8. List five things that you like about being a sales professional:	1. 2. 3. 4. 5.
9. Complete the following sentence: 'A sales **professional** is someone who …'	

The importance of selling – key points

The ratio of salespeople to employees is estimated at 1:40.

Your approach, skill, knowledge, professionalism, personality and empathy are all benefits to the customer.

The future of your company rests with its future customers. Successful salespeople create, jobs, growth, security, careers and opportunity.

Selling rewards success in many ways, such as prestige, money, autonomy, job security, variety, challenge, working with people – remind yourself of these on a daily basis.

A product (or service) is 50 per cent what it is, 50 per cent what it does and 100 per cent the way it is sold.

You are the **business** – you make customers possible, who in turn make pay-days possible.

Consider how you would like to be sold to – work to high professional and ethical standards. Selling is a true profession; it takes years of effort, constant development and skill to excel at selling. **Always be proud to be a salesperson.**

Sell yourself on your job – it makes everything easier: 'the first sale you make is to yourself'.

'A sales professional is someone who sells goods and products that don't come back to customers who do.'

Reproduced from *Sales Training Games*, Graham Roberts-Phelps, Gower, Aldershot 57

4

Models and methods

Overview This collection of training exercises applies proven sales models to the participant's own situation, with the aim of improving skills and knowledge levels.

Process The trainer briefly describes an established model or method regarding a particular aspect of sales or marketing. Participants are then given the time and opportunity to apply the model to their own skills, personality and approach. A general discussion can then be run as appropriate.

Activities Setting your own goals
Key questioning skills
Selling benefits
Most common objections
Closing questions
Pipeline planning
Customer fact-find
Selling by telephone
Rent payers and sleeping giants
The John Todd formula

Setting your own goals

Summary   Participants are encouraged to identify personal and organizational priorities and how to achieve them.

Objectives   structuring goal setting and achievement planning

Materials   Handouts provided, flip chart

Timing   40–50 minutes

Procedure
1. Introduce the exercise by setting the group the following short task.

   Write the question 'What do you want?' on a flip chart. Tell the group they have 60 seconds to make a list of all the things that they want.

   After 60 seconds, ask people to stop writing and go around the group asking each participant to shout out something they want. Query interesting or humorous items for more details.

   Highlight that we can have almost anything we want – the choices are vast. However, the first step is to decide **what we want**, and that means making a decision. This decision often involves deciding **what we don't want**.

2. Ask the group the following questions as a way of generally introducing the theme of goal setting.

   - What experience do you have of goal setting?
   - How often do you set goals? Do you write them down?
   - Do your goals change?
   - Do you have conflicting goals? How do you know what you **really** want?
   - Does everybody have goals?
   - What is the difference between actually wanting something and setting a specific goal?

The following are some commonly held views on goal setting, which may help in your discussion.

- You can't hit a target you can't see.
- Goals give you purpose and focus, and are the key to self-motivation.
- Creating exciting and motivating challenges helps us bring out the best in ourselves and others.
- A goal is a dream taken seriously.
- Goal-setting is the master skill of success, yet less than 5 per cent of people have written goals.
- Goals should be reviewed and checked regularly – like a map on a journey.
- If you don't know where you're going, it doesn't really matter how or if you get there.
- Goals should be 'SMART', that is Specific, Measurable, Achievable, Realistic and Time-bounded.
- Goals can be short term (1, 2 or 3 months) or long term (3, 5 or 10 years).
- You can have goals for all areas of life (work, family and friends, personal and self-development) – they are not just about money.
- Having a goal helps to create a feeling of accomplishment and achievement when we get to where we are going.
- Most people spend more time planning their holidays than they do their lives.

3. Distribute the handouts and ask participants to work through them individually, answering each question as thoroughly as possible. Explain that this should take about 30 minutes. After all, they will spend long enough achieving these goals, so it is worth spending time defining them.

Distribute the handouts and allow 30 minutes.

4. After 30 minutes, ask the group to reassemble and ask each participant to review their examples, comments, thoughts and conclusions. You can encourage discussion with the following questions.

- Do your 'wants' seem clearer and more achievable?
- How does creating milestones affect the goal?

Rather than discussing goals directly, which might be of a personal nature, it might be better to structure the summary around whether the exercise was easy or difficult and whether anyone found anything that surprised them.

Setting your own goals

Make a list of some of the things that you would like to achieve in the next one, two and three years.

Make sure you have a mix of business or work/sales goals, personal goals and family goals. Include anything you would like to achieve, no matter how big or small. Then complete the following tasks.

_____

_____

_____

_____

_____

1. Review your list of goals or 'wants' and target a specific completion date against each goal in your list.
2. Go through your list again and this time mark by each goal one of the following.

   A – for high priority (very important)
   B – for medium priority (important)
   C – for just nice to have

3. List here your top three (A category) goals which have a target date for completion during the next 6–12 months.

   1.
   2.
   3.

cont'd

 Reproduced from *Sales Training Games*, Graham Roberts-Phelps, Gower, Aldershot

Now take each one of your top three A category goals and put them through the questions on the 'Setting your own goals – a worksheet' handout, detailing your answers on a separate piece of paper. If you have time, move on to your other A goals, and then B and C.

Setting your own goals – a worksheet

Goal:

1. How will you know when you have achieved this goal? What will you see, hear or experience?
2. How will having achieved this goal make you feel?
3. Why do you want to achieve it? List some of the reasons.
4. On a scale of 1 to 10 how badly do you want to achieve it (with 10 being the most, 1 the least)?
5. Create a series of milestones or sub-goals that you can aim for over the next 90 days that will take you towards your main goal.
6. Activity goals towards the main goal (with dates):

   i.

   ii.

   iii.

7. What obstacles are you likely to encounter, and how might you overcome them?
8. Decide on one thing, no matter how small, you can do **today**, to start you on your way to this goal – make some notes **now**!

Key questioning skills

Summary   A short input exercise to summarize some key points around sales questioning techniques.

Objectives   summarizing

Materials   Handout provided, flip chart

Timing   20–30 minutes

Procedure
1. Distribute the handout provided and introduce the theme.
2. Make one point at a time, prompting participants to ask questions, contribute relevant past or present examples, check for understanding and discuss each point before moving on. Try to give, or ask participants for, examples and list these on a flip chart.

Although these points are clearly very general, they could easily be customized with relevant examples from your own work environment, procedures and standards.

Key questioning skills

- Never assume anything – ask, find out and clarify.
- Use a structured questioning technique – going from situation … to problems … to implications … to cost-implications.
- Give the customer time to think and reply.
- No problem, need or desire to solve it means no chance of a sale.
- Don't ignore the emotional and 'soft' questions.
- Back-track and summarize and to create a 'sales staircase'.
- The customer will tell you how to sell to them – if you ask the right questions.

Selling benefits

Summary   A discussion exercise around identifying and using features, advantages and benefits.

Objectives   improving communication

Materials   Handout provided, flip chart

Timing   40–60 minutes

Procedure
1. Introduce the exercise by explaining that its purpose is to highlight what benefits a product or service may have and how best to communicate them.
2. Ask the group for definitions of features and benefits. Let the group suggest definitions of each. If participants are new to this concept, or you feel would gain from a refresher, continue by running a short group discussion on the features and benefits of several common products or services. Do this by writing 'Features' on the left hand side of a flip chart and letting participants suggest benefits to be listed on the right hand side.
3. Distribute the first handout and review the definitions of features, advantages and benefits. Discuss examples of linking statements, for example, 'which means that' and 'that's because'.
4. Divide the participants into groups of 2–3. Distribute the second handout and ask the groups to list ten features, with their associated advantages and benefits that could be used in a sales situation.

Distribute the second handout and allow 15 minutes.

5. After 15 minutes, reassemble the main group and take examples. Lead a discussion, using the following questions.

- If you are selling identical products, how could you differentiate between them?
- When faced with a large choice of products or services, with only small perceived differences, what makes **you** buy one over another, or from one shop against another?
- What would persuade your customers?

The points you are looking for are that it is selling specific benefits that makes the difference; specifically, having the benefits made clear or the product explained in relation to our own personal and unique needs and wants is the key. The quality and professionalism of the sales and service that customers receive is also critical, and often a major deciding factor.

1 Selling benefits

- Features (what it is)
- Advantages (what it does) – sometimes known as functions
- Benefits (how it benefits the individual customer – personal benefits)
- 'You' appeal (benefits made personal and specific to the customer's previous established needs, wants and preferences)
- use linking statements such as:
  - 'Which means that …'
  - 'The advantage of this is …'
  - 'Therefore …'
  - 'This means that …'
  - 'This offers you …'
  - 'The benefit to you is …'

2 Selling benefits

Create a list of features, with their associated advantages and benefits that you can use in a sales call or situation.

Feature	Advantages	Benefit
1.		
2.		
3.		
4.		
5.		
6.		
7.		
8.		
9.		
10.		

Most common objections

Summary   Working in small groups, participants practise using the **C**larify, **L**isten, **E**mpathy, **A**nswer, **R**eassure method for tackling common objections to buying.

Objectives improving communication
                inter-personal skills

Materials   Handout provided, flip chart

Timing   40 minutes, plus discussion

Procedure 1. Introduce the exercise by asking participants for examples of the main objections that they hear at any time in the sales cycle – whether trying to get an appointment or asking for a final commitment.
               2. Summarize each example in one or two words each on a flip chart, grouping together similar or repeated objections. You will probably get no more than about eight or nine, maybe fewer per category.
               3. Explain how this shows that 80 per cent of all buying objections fall within the same five or six questions or concerns. Suggest that by identifying these **in advance** and preparing for them, participants can greatly increase their sales effectiveness. They might not be able to close every sale, but it will certainly enable a few more. You could highlight the different types of objections by presenting them in the following way.

               'Real' objections or questions: These are genuine concerns or questions that people need or want to have answered before making a decision. People are not always clear or forthcoming on these, and they often start out as 'put-offs' or false objections.

71

Conditions: These are actual barriers to a sale, such as not having sufficient authority or having no money. (Price is not an objection, but lack of perceived value is.)

False objections: These are just things that people say in the hope of getting rid of salespeople, for example 'I'm too busy', 'I'm just looking', 'I can't afford it' (although lack of budget may be a condition, a statement such as 'too expensive' or 'more expensive' may be a comparative and subjective statement rather than a statement of fact).

- A genuine objection is a sincere buying signal and shows interest.
- Objections are telling you what you've missed and what's important to the customer.
- Selling starts when the customer says 'No'.
- Welcome objections – remain calm and unflustered.

4. Divide the participants into groups of 2–3 and distribute the handouts provided. You could run a quick example with the whole group, based on one of the suggested objections previously given.

Distribute the handout and allow 20–30 minutes.

5. After 20–30 minutes, reassemble the group and ask for examples of objections and the corresponding responses. Ask participants to make additional notes. You can prompt discussion with the following questions.

- Where in the sale do you get which objections?
- Do you always get closing objections?
- Is it possible to prevent or pre-answer objections?

An optional exercise of 30–60 minutes is as follows. Ask participants to return to their groups and role play each objection, with participants taking turns to play the positions of salesperson, customer and observer. Summarize any findings in a short group discussion.

Most common objections

The objective of this exercise is to identify the most commonly encountered buying objections and ways of overcoming them. Of all the buying objections you will encounter, most will be the same five or six basic objections. By identifying these and preparing for them you can greatly increase your sales effectiveness.

1. List your six most commonly encountered objections during the sales process.

1.	2.
3.	4.
5.	6.

2. For each objection in turn identify ways of dealing with the objection using the following steps.

A. **Clarify**

Which question/s would help to uncover any hidden concerns, test the seriousness of the objection and further clarify what the specific and real objection is?

B. **Listen**

How would you actively listen?

C. **Empathy**

Which statement/s would acknowledge empathy and understanding for this objection?

cont'd

D. **Answer**

How could you answer the objections? Perhaps identify features, benefits or examples that could be raised earlier in the sale to pre-empt this objection.

E. **Reassure/recap**

3. Write a phrase to test if the objection has been answered and attempt a trial close if appropriate.

Closing questions

Summary   Competitive brainstorming to generate a list of creative closing questions.

Objectives   generation of ideas
confidence-building
learning techniques

Materials   Handouts provided, flip chart

Timing   30 minutes

Procedure   1.   Introduce the exercise by highlighting that most salespeople close only once or twice, and yet surveys show that most sales are won after the fourth of fifth closing question. Therefore, you need to have several trial or test closing questions to use throughout the sale, and particularly at the end.
2.   Run a short group discussion to list different types of closing and trial closing questions and gain examples of each, also make sure that the group are familiar with the definition of a trial closing question.

Examples of types of closing question are as follows.

● Is that what you are looking for?
● How does that sound to you?
● Would you be able to proceed on that basis?

Deal with the following types of closing questions.

● Assertive close – Would you like to place an order?
● Alternative choice – Black or white?
● Indirect close – Would you like to take it with the carrying case?

75

- Invitation close – Why don't you give it a try?

3. Divide the group into two teams, or groups of 4–6, and distribute the first handout.

Distribute the first handout and allow about 20 minutes.

It may be useful to circulate between the two groups offering ideas and suggestions.

4. After 20 minutes, ask for short group summaries asking each group to read out their lists of questions. You could award small 'prize' to the group with the most questions, and to groups with particularly bizarre or inventive questions.
5. Conclude the exercise by distributing the second handout and asking participants to make a note of any questions that have not been covered in the exercise.

Distribute the second handout.

Commentary You could develop the exercise further with a short discussion about closing in general. The following questions could prompt discussion.

- How do you know when to close?
- Do you ever forget to close and the customer buys anyway?
- What is the difference between being persistent and being a pest?
- Do you think people (including yourself) are good at making buying decisions?
- Why do people procrastinate over making purchasing decisions?

This discussion allows participants to discuss issues of importance to them and learn from others in the group and, of course, from you. The very process of discussing techniques and problems in this way can build confidence and remove performance 'blocks'.

Closing questions

Most salespeople close only once or twice, and yet surveys show that most sales are won after the fourth or fifth closing question.

Therefore, you need to have **lots** of trial or test closing questions to use throughout the sale (particularly at the end).

In your group, think of as many closing and trial closing questions as you can, no matter how bizarre or unusual. You can make them specific to particular products, customers or situations.

1. _____

2. _____

3. _____

4. _____

5. _____

6. _____

7. _____

8. _____

9. _____

10. _____

11. _____

12. _____

13. _____

14. _____

15. _____

Example closing questions

- Will delivery on Tuesday be okay for you?
- Would you be looking to take all 12 cases now, or a staggered delivery?
- What's making you hesitate?
- Is that with or without the external battery charger?
- OK, so what is our next step?
- What do we need to do **now** to get this thing done?
- Shall I check the stock position on that?
- If we could match that price and delivery would that be OK?
- How does that sound to you?
- Cash or cheque?
- Would you prefer to use your own finance or our special leasing terms?
- Do you want to handle the paperwork or shall I?
- If I can just have an order number, I could schedule an installation date for next week.
- Are there are any final questions, or is everything to your satisfaction?
- Would you like to choose from our sweet trolley or can I tempt you with the chef's special?
- What else can I do to help you make this decision?
- What more can I do to make sure that you're happy?
- OK, now is there anything else that I can help you with?
- This is going to look great in your living room, don't you agree?
- You know that you won't find better quality for this price anywhere ... so shall we sort out the paperwork?
- Why don't you give it a try?
- I can have this Agreement Proposal typed and presented by tomorrow morning, how does that sound?
- We have a standard model at £19.95, the deluxe version at £24.95 or the executive model at £34.95, which would you prefer?
- I think that is just what you've been looking for, wouldn't you agree?

cont'd

- What warranty would you like with this?
- When should I set the enrolment date for?
- Should I put these by for you?
- Can I just take down your company details for the order and delivery forms?

Pipeline planning

Summary   Working on their own, participants create a 'Sales Pipeline Plan' to help forecast future short-term business.

Objectives   understanding and forecasting sales

Materials   Handout provided, flip chart, participants will need to have a list of current prospects or customers with them (i.e. those expected to buy within the next 1–3 months)

Timing   20–30 minutes

Procedure
1.   Introduce the exercise by asking if participants have ever experienced a 'roller-coaster' effect on their monthly sales. That is a good 'up' month, invariably followed by a 'down' month. Draw a sine wave type graph on the flip chart. (You might find that the companies or divisions sales figures follow this pattern.)
2.   Run a short discussion as to why participants think that this happens, using the following questions.

   - How does it affect your sales commission?
   - How does it affect the company's cash flow?
   - What are the consequences for stock levels and planning of stock levels/staffing?

3.   Explain this exercise is a way of trying to smooth the graph and build a more consistent and steady approach to building sales.
4.   Distribute the handout provided and ask participants to work individually, completing one pipeline form for each of the next three months, with the most detailed being for the following month's summary.

Distribute the handout and allow 20 minutes.

5.   After 20 minutes, ask participants to form pairs and to discuss any issues or actions arising. Each person in the pair should make sure that the other person's sales forecasts are realistic and the identified actions appropriate. (Alternatively, a sales manager or supervisor outside of the group can perform this task.)

If participants do not have any pre-prepared lists of prospects, then restrict the exercise to the next 30 days, which salespeople should be able to do from memory or their diaries.

A variation on the concluding discussion would be to ask each salesperson to give a short presentation on their sales pipeline.

Pipeline planning

Please complete the following forecast for your current best prospects or accounts.

Name	Details	Value and % chance – Month 1	Value and % chance – Month 2	Value and % chance – Month 3
Dobson & Co.	Replacement copier and new fax machine	£8,300 – 70%	£300 – 25%	

Reproduced from *Sales Training Games*, Graham Roberts-Phelps, Gower, Aldershot

Customer fact-find

Summary An exercise in which small groups of participants work to identify a list of seven key fact-finding questions for use during sales calls.

Objectives preparation/improving questioning techniques
self-analysis

Materials Handout provided

Timing 30–40 minutes, plus discussion

Procedure 1. Introduce the exercise by suggesting that a sales call or appointment is far too precious to leave it to chance or to 'wing-it' in the hope of saying the right things and asking the right questions.

Top salespeople use a well-developed series of questions, which are either gained through experience or careful preparation. Regardless of experience, what they sell or to whom, people do develop their own questions in this way. Point out that often they are not aware of this, but when video-recorded or prompted, they find this to be true. Ask participants if they find themselves using the same questions or phrases in different sales calls. Ask if anyone has ever sat down and worked these questions out in advance (unlikely).

2. Explain that this exercise will help participants review their questioning technique and develop some really effective and well-thought-out questions.
3. Divide the participants into groups of 2–3 and distribute the handout provided.

83

Distribute the handout and allow about 20–30 minutes.

4. After 20–30 minutes, or when everybody has finished (it is important not to rush them, and different levels of groups might take slightly longer than others), reassemble the main group and ask each group to present their seven questions by writing them on the flip chart. Discuss any similarities that arise.

5. Close the exercise by reviewing the following possible questions against those questions offered by the groups and asking for comments.

    i.   What are your main responsibilities and job functions?
    ii. What type of products/solutions have you used in the past?
    iii. What **exactly** led you to choose those products/ services and suppliers?
    iv. How much do you know about us/the product or service? (Note: this is a cue for a short presentation, stating the features, benefits, terms, conditions and USPs (unique selling points) of you and your company, etc.)
    v.   Do you have a budget in mind, when you are looking to make a decision and will anybody else be involved in the choice or decision?
    vi. Which criteria do you apply in selecting this product/service?
    vii. How will you know when these criteria have been fulfilled? OR What has to happen in order for you to feel _____ (the above)?

Participants may want to write down these seven questions alongside their own

Participants would benefit from some prior work on question types and techniques. Alternatively, you could review different types of question (particularly open and closed questions) and listening techniques.

If you are going to run this exercise several times, it is a good idea to take copies of participants' examples and compile a 'master list' which can be distributed at the end.

You might like to role play the questions being used. Participants not actually involved in the role play should be 'observers' – noting if the

questions are effective in gaining information or developing needs and writing any additional questions that the sales consultant used. Review each role play in turn.

Customer fact-find

On a separate sheet of paper, list a series of questions you could ask someone during the **first part** of an **initial sales call**. Aim to generate as many questions as possible.

Now imagine that you are only allowed to ask **seven** main questions throughout the whole appointment and these questions **must** lead you to find out everything you need to know about the customer's needs, wants and preferences. (They may of course lead to connected or subsidiary questions.) For example, 'So tell me all about XYZ Plc, perhaps explaining what you do, and describe a little of how you are organized' could be one of your main questions, which would lead to other questions. Choose the seven main questions from your initial list and write them below.

1. _____

2. _____

3. _____

4. _____

5. _____

6. _____

7. _____

Reproduced from *Sales Training Games*, Graham Roberts-Phelps, Gower, Aldershot

Selling by telephone

Summary   A whole-group exercise in summarizing key skills involved in selling by telephone.

Objectives   reviewing techniques

Materials   Handouts provided, flip chart

Timing   20–30 minutes

Procedure   1. Introduce the exercise by reading and reviewing the summary with the group.
                 2. Distribute the handouts provided and explain that the information is taken from observing and studying successful telephone salespeople and analysing their techniques. Although they might need to be adapted to the individual's own style and sales situation, participants should find an application for virtually all of them in making calls.

Distribute the handouts.

3. Review each of the handouts in turn. Reveal one point at a time, asking participants to give past or present examples, as well as offering those of your own. Discuss each fully before moving on and ask participants to make notes.
4. List any extra comments or ideas on a flip chart.
5. Close the exercise by perhaps showing a video or run a short role-play demonstration involving yourself and another participant, with you acting as salesperson.

Although these points are very general, they could easily be customized with relevant examples from your own work environment, procedures and standards.

Selling by telephone – Key points

- First, focus on a simple objective (your ideal objective), for example to get an appointment.
- Have a 'fall-back' objective, for example to gain information for a call-back.
- Talk slowly and think quickly.
- Be bold and talk with a feeling of command.
- Let the customer hear you smile.
- Ask questions to give you control and time to think.
- Focus on benefits of the meeting not the product/service.
- Trial close and close regularly.
- Make the appointment sound easy, friendly and of benefit to the customer.
- Use objections as a reason to meet.

Selling by telephone – 'T.E.L.E.P.H.O.N.E.S.'

T Three rings
The optimum time to answer a call is between three and five rings. Too quick and you can catch the caller off-guard, any longer and you may cause annoyance.

E Enthusiasm and energy
As the caller can't see your face you have to communicate this by the tone of your voice and the words you use. Keep sentences short, and put a 'bounce' into your voice. Show sincere interest in helping the caller.

L Listen and show you are listening
This means not only asking questions, but also summarizing key points to show that you've understood the caller, and using regular 'aha's to indicate that you are still listening.

E Enunciate and check words
Check for spellings of any word on which you are not clear, especially people's names. Make sure your own speech is crisp, clear and well paced. It is best to speak slightly slower than you would normally.

P Precision
Avoid general points, and make sure you establish precise details. Whether you are taking a message or confirming an order, make sure that you have enough information. For instance, if somebody leaves a message for someone else to call them back, find out what time they will be available.

H Hold button – don't use it
Nobody likes being put on hold, so don't do it unless you really have to. If you do have to, make sure it is for no longer than 30 seconds. Always offer people a choice. Also, avoid asking people to call you back. You should call them back, this way you stay in control.

cont'd

O **Open questions**
Whoever talks dominates the conversation, whoever asks questions controls it. Answer a question with an answer, immediately followed by a question.

N **Notes – take them and read them back to the customer**
Unless you are blessed with a photographic memory, there is a very good chance that will you forget 90 per cent of a call within 60 minutes. Most of us have to ask the caller to repeat their name at the end of a three-minute conversation, because we have forgotten it. Take notes continuously throughout the call and read back the key points to check them with the caller.

E **Eating!**
In a large scale survey of business phone users, the main dislike was the other person eating, drinking, chewing or smoking whilst on the phone. These actions are amplified extremely well down the phone!

S **Summarize at the end of the call**
At the end of every call summarize what has been discussed and what actions are to take place. If it is an important call or if an appointment has been made, a short fax or letter confirming the details is also very professional.

Rent payers and sleeping giants

Summary   A pairs exercise in which participants plot 10 accounts on the Account Planning Matrix and learn how to distinguish between accounts and prioritize their time.

Objectives   analysis
priority-setting

Materials   Handouts provided

Timing   20–25 minutes, plus discussion

Procedure   1. Distribute the handouts provided.

Distribute the handouts.

2. Explain that the matrix is comprised of two variables – account opportunity and competitive position. Review the first handout – the overview – with the whole group.
3. Ask participants to work in pairs and plot up to ten accounts on to the matrix, and then rank them according to priority, based on this approach.

Allow 15–20 minutes.

4. After 15–20 minutes, discuss the findings in a group summary, and explain that this will enable participants to decide which accounts merit the most time and energy. Discussion can be prompted using the following questions.

   ● What account is your number one priority?
   ● Is your time currently being split correctly based on this analysis?
   ● How can you use this approach in planning your sales activity?

Account opportunity matrix – overview

This is a method of account analysis and time allocation known as the 'portfolio model'. It is based on two criteria: account opportunity and competitive position.

Account opportunity includes things such as the account's growth rate, the capacity for your company's goods and services, and its financial health.

Competitive position refers to the strength of the company in that account. Considerations in this section include the account's overall attitude towards suppliers, the past transaction and account history and the strength of the personal relationship.

The term 'call ratio' refers to the approximate amount of time that this category of accounts should be allocated from your total selling time.

The benefits of using the account opportunity matrix are that it allows you to organize and manage your sales time, and also to project the future potential of each and every prospect and customer. It is also very useful in developing a strategic way of thinking about your sales territory and accounts.

Segment 1 'Target Busters'

These are the most attractive of all accounts. They have a high potential and a strong competitive position.

Strategy for selling: Make them your number one priority for sales time allocation and company resources. Call ratio: 45 per cent.

Segment 2 'Sleeping giants'

These are also very attractive accounts. They have a high potential and yet a weak competitive position, and you are probably trailing an established supplier.

cont'd

Strategy for selling: Additional analysis and planning is needed to identify where your competitive position is weak and how it can be improved. Call ratio: 30 per cent.

Segment 3 'Rent payers'

These accounts are moderately attractive. They have a low potential and a strong competitive position.

Strategy for selling: Should receive just enough sales resources to maintain competitive position and as source of referrals. Call ratio: 20 per cent.

Segment 4 'Bottom drawer'

These are the least attractive of all accounts. They have a low potential and a weak competitive position.

Strategy for Selling: Service by telephone or mail, or wait for them to call you. Call ratio: 5 per cent.

Account planning

Plot your current customers and prospects on this account opportunity matrix.

	LOW account opportunity	HIGH account opportunity
HIGH competitive advantage	Segment 3 'Rent payers'	Segment 1 'Target busters'
LOW competitive advantage	Segment 4 'Bottom drawer'	Segment 2 'Sleeping giants'

The John Todd formula

Summary   Participants learn the John Todd formula (sales productivity ratio), based around call rate, order value and closing percentage, and practise applying it to measure their own sales performance.

Objectives   introduction to sales productivity
goal-setting

Materials   Handouts provided, flip chart, participants should have the following three key pieces of data for the previous month/period: total number of calls, number of orders (expressed as a percentage), average order value

Timing   30–40 minutes

Procedure   1.   Introduce the exercise by stating it is based on the John Todd formula which goes back many years. It is a useful and reasonably reliable way of looking at three sales result variables (sales calls made, average order value and number of orders taken) and producing a comparative figure, which can be used to assess relative sales productivity.
2.   Relate the story of three salespeople. Feel free to elaborate on the basic facts:

- The first made endless calls and collected scores of small orders on a regular basis.
- The second spent most of the week on the golf course, and made a few well-placed calls to major customers.
- The third didn't make lots of calls, or get many big orders, but seemed have more customers than the other two salespeople put together.

Ask participants to comment on which salesperson was the

most productive and why. Encourage discussion by challenging initial assumptions. Explain that often salespeople, particularly the good ones, will succeed by taking several large orders, which can mask a weakness in call consistency, volume or orders. The John Todd formula takes all three into account and helps sales managers make valid comparisons between salespeople. Distribute the first handout and work through the points with the participants.

Distribute the first handout.

3. Distribute the second handout and ask participants to work either individually or in pairs. Offer assistance to any participants who are having problems.

Distribute the second handout and allow 15 minutes.

4. After 15 minutes, or when everybody has finished, ask each participant to read out their scores. Lead a short group discussion around the following questions, making a note of key points that arise on a flip chart.

    ● Is this formula a good measure of sales productivity?
    ● How well can it be used to compare results between salespeople, branches or divisions?
    ● What does it tell us about our sales activity?
    ● Which of the three variables (sales calls, order value, number of orders) is it most important to increase?
    ● Which do you think is the easiest to increase?

5. Distribute the third handout and ask participants to complete their action plans with some short-term goals based on what they have learnt from completing this exercise. Allow 10 minutes.

Distribute the third handout and allow 10 minutes.

The John Todd formula

This is a useful and reasonably reliable way of looking at three sales result variables:

- sales calls made,
- average order value, and
- number of orders taken.

Calculating these together produces a comparative figure, which can be used to assess relative sales productivity. It is also known as the Sales Productivity Rating (SPR).

Sales productivity rating =

Sales call/appointments in period (A)

x

Percentage result in orders (X%)

x

Average order value

÷

Number of working days in period (D)

For example, if a salesperson called George made 25 calls in a month, with 7 orders, and an average order value of £5,400, his SPR would be 7560 (given 20 working days).

How would this compare to George's rival John, who has made 21 calls and taken 8 orders with an average value of £5,600 in the same period?

Calculation examples:

George $(25 \times 28\% \times 5{,}400) \div 20 = 1{,}890$

John $(21 \times 38\% \times 5{,}600) \div 20 = 2{,}234$

The higher the rating, the greater the sales productivity.

📑   # Sales productivity rating

For your last full calendar sales month, complete the following.

Appointments/Sales calls made (A): _____
Number resulting in order (B): _____
Therefore closing percentage is: _____ % (X%)
(B divided by A multiplied by 100%)
Your average order value: _____
Days worked (D): _____
Calculate your SPR.

For your own SPR, and for that of George and John, consider the following questions.

● What effect would a 20 per cent increase in order value have?
● What effect would a 20 per cent increase in calls made have?
● What effect would a 20 per cent increase in orders taken have?
● What would be the effect of all three of the above happening at once?

Sales productivity rating – action plan

1. Three things I could do in the next 30 days to increase my call rate by 20 per cent:

   1. _____
   2. _____
   3. _____

2. Three things I could do in the next 30 days to increase my closing rate or orders taken as a percentage of total calls (also by 20 per cent):

   1. _____
   2. _____
   3. _____

3. Three things I could do in the next 30 days to increase my average order value:

   1. _____
   2. _____
   3. _____

Commitment to achieve these changes.

I hereby make a solid commitment to work consistently and creatively to achieve the above.

Signed _____   Date _____

5

Quizzes and questionnaires

Purpose   Quizzes seem to be a really popular addition to any sales course, especially if a spirit of friendly rivalry is established. This is best done by dividing the group into two or three teams and awarding points for each answer. You can also easily develop your own quizzes expanding upon the suggestions here. Many answers to the questionnaires are subjective (rather than right or wrong) and so are to be compared and discussed.

Process   The exercises are similar in their format and duration and require little preparation.

Activities   Product knowledge
Company knowledge
Presentation skills
Questioning skills
Rapport building
Objection handling
Sales time management
Prospecting

Product knowledge

Summary A simple product knowledge quiz that makes a good ice-breaker or warm-up exercise. It can also be used as a useful end-of-course competency test.

Objectives self-analysis/review

Materials Handout provided

Timing 30 minutes

Procedure
1. Introduce the exercise by highlighting that knowing your company and knowing your product are two absolutely fundamental prerequisites of being a professional salesperson. Work through the following key points.

   ● You have to be confident that there is no question a customer could ask that you would not know or could not find the answer to.
   ● Knowing about your market, competitors and customer's business is all part of product knowledge.
   ● Superior product knowledge is an edge.
   ● You must study your product and market place regularly; it will be an investment.
   ● Excellent product knowledge creates confidence and builds credibility.

2. Distribute the handout provided and set a time-limit of 15 minutes.

Distribute the handout and allow 15 minutes.

3. After 15 minutes, ask participants to swap papers and to

compare each other's responses. Review each question in turn, dealing with any issues that arise.

You might want to supplement or replace the standard quiz with your own specific set of questions. Be sure to adjust the time accordingly.

Product knowledge

Question	Answer
1. What are your three best selling products/services?	1. 2. 3.
2. What is your worst selling or performing product/service?	
3. What product/service do you enjoy selling the most and why?	

For each of the three best selling products/services listed in 1., give three reasons or factors that you believe contribute to their success:

Product/service 1: _____
Factors/reasons for success:

Product/service 2: _____
Factors/reasons for success:

Product/service 3: _____
Factors/reasons for success:

Company knowledge

Summary   This quiz focuses on how much participants know about their own company and makes a useful ice-breaker or warm-up exercise.

Objectives   self-analysis/review

Materials   Handout provided

Timing   30 minutes

Procedure

1. Introduce the exercise by highlighting that knowing your company and knowing your product are two absolutely fundamental prerequisites of being a professional salesperson.
2. Distribute the handout provided and set a time-limit of 15 minutes.

Distribute the handout and allow 15 minutes.

3. After 15 minutes, ask participants to swap papers and to compare responses. Review each question in turn, dealing with any issues that may arise. The following questions could be used to prompt discussion.

    ● What benefits are there for you as a salesperson in knowing your company well?
    ● What benefits are there for the customer?
    ● How can you find out more about your company? Which sources could provide information?

You might want to supplement or replace the standard quiz with your own specific set of questions. Be sure to adjust the time accordingly.

Company knowledge

Write answers on a separate sheet of paper.

Question

1. What is the name of your managing director/chief executive?

2. What was the company's turnover for the last financial year?

3. When was the company established?

4. What are three interesting (to a customer) facts about your company?

5. How many people are currently employed in your company?

6. What three things impress you most about your company?

7. What is your company's greatest strength?

8. What is your company's greatest weakness?

cont'd

9. Why should a customer buy from your company (as opposed to a competitor)? List as many reasons as you can.

10. Can you name:
    the company's best selling product/division?

    the company's largest customers (by sales volume)?

    the company's number one competitors?

11. In about 30 words, describe the company, as you might do to a customer.

12. What are three other subsidiary companies or divisions of the company?

Presentation skills

Summary   A short warm-up or ice-breaker based on the various skills of presentation.

Objectives   self-evaluation

Materials   Handout provided

Timing   20–30 minutes

Procedure   1.   Distribute the handout and set a time-limit of 15 minutes.

Distribute the handout and allow 15 minutes.

2.   After 15 minutes, or when everybody has finished, ask participants to swap papers and to compare each other's responses. Review each question in turn, dealing with any issues that may arise. You could prompt discussion with the following questions.

- What level of agreement is there as to 'good' and 'bad' qualities of presenters and presentations?
- How much of a good presentation is preparation and practice and how much depends on the personality of the presenter?

You might want to supplement or replace the standard quiz with your own specific set of questions. Be sure to adjust the time accordingly.

Presentation skills

Question	Answer
1. Name three people who have impressed you as persuasive or skilled presenters.	1. 2. 3.
2. What are the qualities they had that particularly impressed you?	
3. Which do you believe to be the most important of these two factors? Give your reasons.	(a) Knowing your subject (b) Appearing confident and presenting skilfully
4. What is the most important thing in giving a presentation?	(a) Making best use of OHPs and flip charts (b) Impressing people with your presentation ability (c) Impressing people with your subject knowledge (d) Impressing people with long words (e) Having a good time (f) Motivating people to take action or change ideas

cont'd

Reproduced from *Sales Training Games*, Graham Roberts-Phelps, Gower, Aldershot 109

5. What do you dislike most in seeing other people present?	
6. Which of your presentation skills would you like to be able to improve upon?	
7. How are you going to do this and create opportunities to practise your presentation skills?	

Questioning skills

Summary   A good exercise based on questioning skills for introducing, summarizing, reviewing or linking course segments.

Objectives   self-analysis
development of interpersonal skills

Materials   Handout provided

Timing   30–40 minutes

Procedure   1.   Distribute the handout and set a time-limit of 10 minutes. Discuss the following types of questions.

- Tell me – general information gathering, often not specific, such as 'Tell me about your current car'.
- Hard fact – establish true facts, such as 'when did you purchase it?'.
- Soft fact – gather more qualitive information, such as 'what do you like/dislike about it?'.
- Disturbing questions – enquire about problems and implications, such as 'Have you had to replace any expensive parts yet?'.

Distribute the handout and allow 10 minutes.

2.   After 10 minutes, review each question in turn, dealing with any issues that arise.
3.   Ask two participants to role play their questions in front of the group, for about 5–10 minutes. The person playing the customer should portray a typical, realistic customer. Repeat as time permits, with a short discussion after each role play (highlighting the importance of questions within the sales process).

111

You might want to supplement or replace the standard quiz with your own specific set of questions. Be sure to adjust the time accordingly.

Questioning skills

Question	Answer
1. Give two examples of open questions that you could use in a sales conversation.	1. 2.
2. Give two examples of 'tell me' questions that you might use in a sales call.	1. 2.
3. Give two examples of hard-fact questions that you might use in a sales call.	1. 2.
4. Give two examples of soft-fact questions that you might use in a sales call.	1. 2.
5. Give two examples of disturbing questions that you might use in a sales call.	1. 2.
6. Give two examples of buying criteria questions that you might use in a sales call.	1. 2.
7. Give two examples of consequence questions that you might use in a sales call.	1. 2.
8. Give two examples of trial closing or summary questions that you might use in a sales call.	1. 2.

Rapport building

Summary A simple exercise on the skills of approaching customers and rapport-building.

It is a good activity for introducing, summarizing, reviewing or linking segments. It can also be used as an ice-breaker, a warm-up exercise, or a follow-on from a training video.

Objectives self-analysis
development of interpersonal skills

Materials Handout provided

Timing 25–30 minutes

Procedure 1. Distribute the handout and set a time-limit of 15 minutes.

Distribute the handout and allow 15 minutes.

2. After 15 minutes, ask participants to swap papers and to compare each other's responses. Review each question in turn, discussing fully any issues that arise.

You might want to supplement or replace the standard quiz with your own specific set of questions. Be sure to adjust the time accordingly.

Rapport building

Question	Answer
1. Why is rapport important to success in selling?	
2. Can you sell to people you don't like?	
3. How do you know when you have a rapport with someone?	
4. Name five things that you can do in the first five minutes of any meeting or conversation to begin to build rapport.	1. 2. 3. 4. 5.
5. Why is the first five minutes of any sales call so important?	
6. Complete this sentence: 'People like people who are …'	
7. Do you believe it is possible to get along with anybody? Give your reasons.	Yes/No/Not sure

cont'd

8. When meeting or talking to a customer for the first time, which is more important:	(a) your appearance (b) the way you talk (c) your body language (d) the company's reputation (e) your hairstyle
9. If somebody was very abrupt and aggressive, how would you try to sell to them?	

Objection handling

Summary   A short competitive quiz on handling objections. It is useful for introducing, summarizing, reviewing or linking segments, and can also be used as an ice-breaker or warm-up exercise.

Objectives   self-analysis
development of interpersonal skills

Materials   Handout provided

Timing   25–30 minutes

Procedure   1. Distribute the handout and set a time-limit of 15 minutes.

Distribute the handout and allow 15 minutes.

2. After 15 minutes, ask participants to swap papers and to compare each other's responses. Review each question in turn, discussing fully any issues that arise.

You might want to supplement or replace the standard quiz with your own specific set of questions. Be sure to adjust the time accordingly.

Objection handling

Statement	Answer
1. A genuine and specific objection is a sincere buying signal and shows interest.	True or false?
2. What do objections tell you about the customer's stage in the buying/sales process?	
3. 'Selling starts when the customer says "No".' What does this statement mean to you?	
4. 'Price is not an objection, but lack of perceived value is.' Do you agree with this statement?	
5. What should be your initial reaction upon encountering an objection?	
6. What is the difference between a 'condition' and an objection?	
7. What is the difference between a 'real' objection and a 'false' objection?	
8. What does a price objection tell you?	
9. What does a delay or a 'think about it' objection tell you?	

Sales time management

Summary   A good ice-breaker or warm-up activity for linking segments and to focus on the key elements of good sales time management.

Objectives   self-analysis

Materials   Handout

Timing   25–30 minutes

Procedure   1.   Introduce the exercise by highlighting that making the best use of our sales time is not a one-off thing, but more a series of constant minor improvements and a constant striving to sell more in less time.
2.   Distribute the handout and set a time-limit of 15 minutes.

Distribute the handout and allow 15 minutes.

3.   After 15 minutes, ask participants to swap papers and to mark each other's. Review each question in turn, dealing with any issues that may arise.
4.   Ask participants to review their answers and highlight:

● three things they currently do that are strong time management traits,
● three areas they could improve upon, and
● three things they are going to do immediately to better manage their time and sales activity.

Sales time management

Please complete the following questionnaire as honestly as you can, circling the response you feel most appropriate. 1 = Never, 2 = Occasionally, 3 = Usually, 4 = Often, 5 = Always

Question	Answer
1. I start each day by reviewing or writing my daily schedule.	1 2 3 4 5
2. I am able to easily set priorities based on sales results.	1 2 3 4 5
3. I take time to plan ahead and regularly review my calls or appointments.	1 2 3 4 5
4. I start work on the least favourite task first.	1 2 3 4 5
5. I am able to avoid trivial tasks.	1 2 3 4 5
6. I avoid wasting time with interruptions and office socializing.	1 2 3 4 5
7. I arrive early for appointments and allow for travel delays.	1 2 3 4 5
8. I avoid wasting time reading newspapers or magazines when I could be selling. (Tip: be selective when reading, scan and select.)	1 2 3 4 5
9. I carry things with me that I can work on when I have a few minutes to spare.	1 2 3 4 5
10. I am able to participate in tasks easily.	1 2 3 4 5

cont'd

Question	Answer
11. I deal with paperwork as it arrives and use the principle of 'touch paper only once'.	1 2 3 4 5
12. I have an organized prospect and sales tracking system, and carefully log call-backs and notes on each customer contact.	1 2 3 4 5
13. I get sales reports done on time, and take time to analyse my sales results on a periodic basis.	1 2 3 4 5
14. I spend as much time as possible getting face-to-face with customers.	1 2 3 4 5
15. I make time to exercise regularly.	1 2 3 4 5
16. I feel in control of my sales pipeline and work schedule.	1 2 3 4 5
17. I never take on more than I can easily or comfortably accomplish.	1 2 3 4 5
18. I regularly set and review challenging goals for myself.	1 2 3 4 5
19. My call-rate is well above the average for my sales team.	1 2 3 4 5
20. I spend scheduled time every day or week prospecting for new business.	1 2 3 4 5

What your score means:

Less than 30
Your time management needs to be sharper

30–60
This is OK, more self-discipline and application is needed in some areas

60 or more
Role-model material!

Prospecting

Summary   This activity on prospecting skills can be used for introducing, summarizing, reviewing or linking segments. It can also be used as an ice-breaker or warm-up exercise.

Objectives   self-analysis

Materials   Handout provided

Timing   30 minutes

Procedure   1.   Distribute the handout and set a time-limit of 15 minutes.

Distribute the handout and allow 15 minutes.

2.   After 15 minutes, ask participants to swap papers and to compare each other's responses.
3.   Review each question in turn, dealing with any issues that may arise. Close the exercise with a short discussion on any points arising from the questions, and a short review of the importance of prospecting.

You can prompt discussion with the following questions.

● How can you improve your prospecting approach?
● What benefits are there to the company?

You might want to supplement or replace the standard quiz with your own specific set of questions. Be sure to adjust the time accordingly.

📄 Prospecting

1. Which is the best source for self-generated new leads?	(a) Old prospects/leads (b) Cold-calling (c) Referrals from existing customers (d) Stealing other people's accounts
2. Why do you feel that many salespeople are reluctant to prospect or make cold calls?	
3. How do you think this is best overcome?	
4. Why is it important to schedule prospecting regularly on an on-going basis?	
5. How many **new** prospects do you need every week/month to sustain a good sales pipeline?	
6. How do you think you could increase this?	
7. What is your conversion ratio from leads/cold-calls to orders?	
8. Is there one thing you could do to increase this?	

cont'd

9. Name five sources of locating new prospects.	1. 2. 3. 4. 5.
10. Your monthly review of potential sales and prospects shows that you are lacking new leads. What do you do?	(a) Send out a small mail-shot to old prospects/leads (b) Pick up a trade-directory/customer list and start cold-calling (c) Contact your best customers and try to sell them more (d) Do nothing and hope for the best
11. List three benefits to you that arise from successful prospecting.	1. 2. 3.
12. Describe the steps that you would take when starting out on a completely new territory, or with a new product, with no existing leads or existing customers.	

6

Group energizers

Purpose   Group energizers can re-charge a session, marking a change of topics or pace, or a lively interlude.

Process   The exercises vary in their format and duration, although all require little preparation and most last only a few minutes.

Activities   Discussion group
What do you like about selling?
The easiest job in the world!
Personal sales history
Pirate raid
My greatest sale
My worst sales appointment
Top five sales qualities
Selling paper clips
Wordsearches and crosswords

Discussion group

Summary   A group discussion exercise with nine separate trigger topics on working effectively in sales. A flexible exercise that can slot into a session to take up any extra time.

Objectives   generating ideas/discussion
sharing viewpoints

Materials   Flip chart

Timing   20–30 minutes, plus discussion

Procedure
1. Introduce the exercise by explaining that this is an excellent format for developing ideas, reinforcing learning points and encouraging self-analysis. It is also a very good way of accessing and sharing the knowledge, ideas and expertise of more experienced or successful salespeople with others in the group.
2. Write the following trigger question on a flip chart. 'What advice would you give to someone just starting their first day in sales?' Read it out to the group and ask them to write it down.
3. Divide participants into groups of 4–8 and ideally use different rooms for their discussions.
4. After 20 minutes ask for the group summary presentations which will also consider the consequences of the main points to them as salespeople.
5. You can run the same process using any of the following trigger questions.

    ● Salespeople often have a poor image in business, certainly compared to other professions. Why do you think this is and how can it be countered?
    ● What current trends do you perceive in your market

place and in the buying patterns of your customers?

- What is most important to your customers and how do you present/highlight this with regard to your product/services?
- What does success mean to you? How do you know when you're selling well? How do you know when you're the best?
- How important is goal setting and positive thinking to you in your sales career? Give specific examples.
- What has been your single greatest achievement in sales in the past year/in your career? What are you most proud of about what you do?
- What do you like most about being a sales professional? How do you motivate yourself through the tough days and when you miss your targets?
- List the top **five** skills which you think are the most important in order to be consistently successful as a salesperson, giving reasons.

There is a hidden benefit to this activity in that it gives participants an opportunity to practise group communication and discussion skills.

What do you like about selling?

Summary   A session starter or introduction exercise in which participants, working in pairs, interview one another to identify their selling likes and dislikes.

Objectives   group familiarization

Materials   Flip chart

Timing   20–30 minutes

Procedure   1. Divide participants into pairs and ask them to interview each other in order to find out a short history about their partner. They should find out the answer to the following question, which you then write on the flip chart

'What do you like most about selling and what do you like least?'

2. After 10 minutes (5 minutes each), ask each participant in turn to present a brief summary of their colleague, together with their 'likes' and 'dislikes'. Summarize these points on the flip chart as you go around the group.

Commentary   You might like to add your own example at the end of the exercise.

In his book *How to Master the Art of Selling* (see Further reading on page 251), Tom Hopkins lists things he likes about selling: freedom, autonomy, money, creativity, a sense of achievement on a daily basis, the challenge, the fact that there are never two days the same, the constant learning and self-development. You could expand these themes, relating them to the participants' own notes.

The easiest job in the world!

Summary   An introductions exercise based on a trigger question: 'What do you think would be the easiest/most difficult sales job in the world?'

Objectives   group familiarization

Materials   Flip chart

Timing   20–30 minutes

Procedure
1. Divide the participants into pairs and ask them to interview each other to find out a short history about their partner. They should also find out the answer to the following question, which you then write on a flip chart.

   'What do you think would be the easiest sales job in the world, and what do you think would be the most difficult?'

   These could be real or imaginary jobs. An example of each might be selling bottled water in the desert and ice-cream to Eskimos!
2. After 10 minutes (5 minutes each), ask each participant in turn to present a brief summary of their colleague, together with their answer to the question. They should make it as interesting and relevant as possible. (You might like to add your own example after the participants.)
3. Conclude the exercise by running a short group discussion around the following question, making a note of key points that arise on the flip chart.

   - Are there such things as 'products that sell themselves'?
   - Are there any products or markets that are easier than any others?

Personal sales history

Summary   An introductions exercise that focuses on 'highlights from your sales career'.

Objectives   group familiarization

Materials   Flip chart

Timing   20 minutes

Procedure

1. Divide the participants into pairs and ask them to interview each other to find out some personal facts about their colleague (such as where they live, their age and family). They should also find out the response to the following question, which you then write on a flip chart.

   'What are the highlights from your sales career?'

2. After 10 minutes (5 minutes each) ask each participant in turn to present a brief summary of their colleague, together with their answer to the question. They should make it as interesting and relevant as possible. (You might like to add your own example at the end.)

3. Conclude the exercise by running a short group discussion around the following questions, making a note of key points that arise on the flip chart.

   - How many people started their careers in another profession and moved into sales?
   - How many people started selling in different products/ services?
   - How were they able to transfer these skills across?
   - Are there any patterns in people's sales careers, and what effect did changing products, managers, economic conditions have on their progression?

Pirate raid

Summary   A classic, challenging and competitive ice-breaker, in which two teams are invited to search for and collect items with which they must return to the training room.

Objectives   developing persuasive and creative skills
lateral thinking
team work

Materials   Handouts provided

Timing   20–30 minutes

Procedure   1.   Divide participants into two teams and distribute handouts A and B provided – one to each team.

Distribute the handouts and allow 15–20 minutes.

2.   After 20 minutes count up the items each team has collected (one point for every item collected and one point for every minute under 15 minutes, but only if all items are collected). Discuss how the various items were obtained and make sure that any items 'borrowed' are returned!

This activity asks participants to 'raid' and 'plunder' the training venue or nearby shops to obtain items from a prepared list. It doesn't matter if some of the items are unobtainable, or cannot be found in the time-limit, this is part of the fun. This activity, if run at the beginning of the course, will get participants working together, and should show you a little about some of the personalities.

Make sure that all items are returned, and if using a hotel check with the duty manager before, and perhaps after, the exercise that there are no problems.

Pirate raid A

As a test of your powers of persuasion, creativity and lateral thinking, collect as many of the items listed in 15 minutes or less. One point will be awarded for every item collected, and one bonus point for every minute under 15 minutes (but only if all items are collected).

- some foreign currency
- a cheque for a million pounds
- a boiled sweet
- the name and address of a complete stranger (in their handwriting)
- a piece of underwear
- a cooking utensil
- the price of a Ford Escort
- a car number plate
- a toilet roll
- a coin dated before 1980
- a 50 pound note
- the telephone number of the British Embassy in Paris
- the full name and date of birth of your managing director

Pirate raid B

As a test of your powers of persuasion, creativity and lateral thinking, collect as many of the items listed in 15 minutes or less. One point will be awarded for every item collected, and one bonus point for every minute under 15 minutes (but only if all items are collected).

- some foreign currency
- a cheque for a million pounds
- a piece of fruit
- the name and address of a complete stranger (in their handwriting)
- a flower
- a workshop tool
- the price of a dozen eggs
- a sign or notice
- a very old newspaper or magazine
- a coin dated before 1980
- a 50 pound note
- the telephone number of the French Embassy in London
- the full name and date of birth of your youngest employee

My greatest sale

Summary An ice-breaker exercise in which participants recall and learn from their greatest sales experience. It can be used to introduce any skills-based activity or a discussion on sales skills, not just as a course introduction or an ice-breaker.

Objectives self-reflection

Materials Flip chart

Timing 40 minutes

Procedure

1. Introduce the exercise by running a short group discussion around the following questions, making a note of key points that arise on a flip chart.

   - Why are some sales more successful than others?
   - Why are some easier than others?

   The outcome of this is, of course, that it is very difficult to generalize, as each sale is completely different, although some general points will begin to emerge such as planning, team-work, not making mistakes and general professionalism.

2. Explain that in this exercise participants will recall a successful sale and try to identify why it was successful, and then see if there are any common elements across the group.

3. Divide the participants into groups of 3–4. Write the phrase 'My greatest sale' on the flip chart in large letters. Ask each of the small groups to recall one of their 'greatest sale' stories, making some notes on the event, identifying some of the reasons why they think the sale was successful and its particular personal significance.

4. After 15 minutes, ask each participant in turn to recall their

greatest sale (allow about 2–3 minutes each). As participants describe their experiences, identify key elements and contributing factors and record them on the flip chart. You might include the following factors.

- Preparation
- Took time to understand the customer
- The product was very well suited to the customer's needs
- Persistence; never gave up
- Enthusiasm

If participants offer any vague definitions, such as 'luck' or 'customer just placed the order', try to identify some key skills or behaviours that may have contributed, by questioning further. Getting participants to recall the sale step-by-step is often a good way of doing this, making sure that they don't generalize about any important elements.

You might like to start or end the activity by recalling a particularly memorable sale of your own.

My worst sales appointment

Summary   An ice-breaker exercise in which participants analyse their worst sales appointment.

Objectives self-reflection

Materials   Handout provided, flip chart

Timing   40 minutes

Procedure   1. Introduce the exercise by running a short group discussion around the following questions, making a note of key points that arise on a flip chart.

- Have you had a recent sales call that went really badly?
- What is the worst thing that ever happened to you on a sales call?
- Why does something work well in one instance, and not so well in another? Can you think of any examples?

The outcome of this is, of course, that it is very difficult to generalize, as each sale is completely different, although there are often common elements.

2. Explain that in this exercise they are going to recall a lost or difficult sale and try to identify why it was so, and then see if there are any common elements across the group.

Be sure to emphasize that this is not an exercise in laying blame or making people feel inadequate (they have probably done that already!), but an objective look to see what can be learned and applied in the future.

3. Divide the participants into groups of 3–4. Write the phrase 'My worst sales appointment' on the flip chart in large letters. Ask the small groups to recall one of their 'worst sales appointment' stories, making some notes on the event,

identifying some of the reasons why the sale was unsuccessful and its particular personal significance.

4.   After 15 minutes ask each participant in turn to recall their worst sales appointment (allow about 2–3 minutes each). As participants describe their experiences, identify key elements and contributing factors and record them on the flip chart. You might include the following factors.

- Lack of skill
- Too rushed
- Didn't listen; talked too much
- Poor preparation; unqualified customer
- Salesperson didn't believe in product
- Poor product knowledge
- Lack of rapport with customer

If participants offer any vague definitions, such as 'luck' or 'customer just wasn't interested', try to identify some key skills or behaviours that may have contributed, by questioning further. Getting participants to recall the sales appointment step-by-step is often a good way of doing this, making sure that they don't generalize about any important elements.

5.   Distribute the handout provided and ask participants to consider making a list of positive action points they can use in the future to apply any lessons learned.

This exercise can be combined with the previous one to create a longer activity that explores or contrasts the differences between successful and less successful calls or sales. You might like to start the activity by recalling a particularly embarrassing experience of your own. After giving a short overview and description, ask participants why they think the sale or appointment might have been such a flop.

It is important the participants finish the exercise with a set of action points (things to do differently next time), rather than a list of things that they have done wrong.

My worst sales appointment – action plan

The most important things that I have learned from this session are:

How I can use these to improve my sales skills:

Other key ideas to implement:

Actions	By when/how
1.	
2.	
3.	

Top five sales qualities

Summary A small group discussion exercise in which participants identify the top five skills or qualities of a successful salesperson.

Objectives generating ideas and discussion
sharing viewpoints
self-analysis

Materials Flip chart

Timing 20–30 minutes

Procedure 1. Write the following trigger question on a flip chart and read it out to the group.

'In order of importance list the top **five** skills or qualities which you think are necessary in order to be consistently successful as a salesperson, giving your reasons.'

Ask the participants to write it down.

2. Divide participants into discussion groups of 3–8 and ideally use different rooms.
3. After 10 minutes, ask a spokesperson from each group to present the main points of the discussion. Allow each group about 3–5 minutes, with extra time for discussion as appropriate.

As well as being a very good way of accessing and sharing the knowledge, ideas and expertise of more experienced or successful salespeople within the group, there is also a hidden benefit – it gives participants an opportunity to practise group communication and discussion skills.

Selling paper clips

Summary A warm-up exercise to explore the difference between feature and benefit presentations, in which participants are asked to sell a paper clip to the trainer. It is a good ice-breaker, particularly with inexperienced salespeople.

Objectives determining benefits

Materials Paper clip, flip chart

Timing 30 minutes

Procedure

1. Do not outline the session objectives or offer any suggestions as to the point of this exercise at the beginning. Simply hand one member of the group an ordinary paper clip and ask him or her to give a short sales presentation of not more than one minute.

   After a minute, or when the person has finished (which is more usual), take the paper clip and hand it to another person, without any comment at all, and repeat the instruction exactly.

   Repeat this, without comment or reply to any responses you are given, five or six times. By this time, the group will become curious as to what the point is.

2. Most people, when confronted with this exercise for the first time, will simply **describe** what a paper clip is, not what it **does**. If any participant spots this and presents the benefits of the paper clip and how useful it can be, simply continue to another participant without comment or acknowledgement. The aim is to get about 80–90 per cent 'descriptions' and one or two 'benefit presentations', if you are lucky.

   Highlight, that out of the people you asked only a few actually mentioned what it actually **did**, not just what it **was**.

It is a piece of bent wire! However, it must be one of the most widely used, indispensable and successful products in the world.

3. Using the following questions encourage group discussion.

- If you were the customer, which sales presentation:
    Explained what the product is?
    Explained what the product did?
- If you had never seen this product, would you want to buy it?
- If all the salespeople were selling identical products at identical prices, who would you buy from and why?

4. Summarize the discussion by noting the key points on the flipchart. These might include that:

- Even the most simple product can have big benefits,
- Unless you communicate the benefits to the customer, there aren't any,
- What something is (that is a piece of bent metal) need not bear any relation to what it can do, or its success as a product.

An optional additional exercise is to develop creative and lateral thinking in relation to ordinary products or services. This can be done by continuing with the theme of the humble paper clip.

Divide the participants into two groups and set each the task of thinking of as many uses for a paper clip as they can, with the team getting the most being deemed the 'winner'. This exercise often highlights some bizarre applications, but it is not uncommon for one or both groups to miss the obvious, namely 'clipping pieces of paper together'. Watch out for this and watch participants' faces when you point this out!

Wordsearches and crosswords

Summary   Four short sales-related wordsearch and crossword puzzles. These are useful as ice-breaker or warm-up exercises.

Procedure   Choose which puzzle to use for the exercise. If you choose a wordsearch you could hand out both the wordsearch chart and the list of target words. Alternatively, you could simply distribute the wordsearch chart and ask the participants to find as many words related to sales jargon as possible.

1. When you distribute the handout(s) to the participants, set a time-limit of 10 minutes.

Distribute the handout(s) and allow 10 minutes.

2. After 10 minutes, ask the participants to swap papers and to mark each other's. Consider awarding a small prize to those with the highest marks, if not a round of applause will suffice.

Sales jargon wordsearch

A	O	X	B	C	P	R	O	P	O	S	A	L	N	P
H	P	C	G	O	S	S	Y	C	B	C	Y	E	O	F
Y	M	P	Q	M	N	E	I	F	J	S	L	S	I	D
H	A	D	O	M	T	U	R	N	E	W	D	O	T	C
C	R	R	I	I	X	Y	S	U	C	C	K	E	S	E
T	G	E	W	S	N	E	G	O	T	I	A	T	E	E
I	I	F	T	S	C	T	X	I	I	A	R	J	U	N
P	N	F	C	J	O	M	B	O	J	E	R	Q	P
O	S	O	E	O	G	D	U	E	N	M	Y	F	T	A
A	F	C	P	N	L	M	P	N	N	A	U	T	V	Z
N	Q	A	S	K	E	D	P	T	T	B	F	C	P
H	T	V	O	Q	U	B	C	U	L	Y	B	D	N	H
E	U	F	R	H	P	Q	B	A	K	I	W	H	E	O
T	R	O	P	P	A	R	W	R	L	F	M	T	A	G
G	T	Y	R	E	F	E	R	R	A	L	X	N	S	Y

Reproduced from *Sales Training Games*, Graham Roberts-Phelps, Gower, Aldershot 143

Sales jargon wordsearch – word list

Appointment	Needs
Benefit	Negotiate
Bonus	Objection
Buyer	Offer
Close	Pitch
Coldcall	Proposal
Commission	Prospect
Discount	Question
Features	Rapport
Margin	Referral

Top companies wordsearch

G	E	N	E	R	A	L	M	O	T	O	R	S	P	C
M	I	C	R	O	S	O	F	T	L	L	O	Y	D	S
E	E	O	Y	Q	Z	U	Z	K	E	U	M	A	I	K
Y	X	C	Q	O	C	S	E	T	N	N	I	L	I	Q
S	X	A	F	O	R	D	C	S	O	I	R	C	Y	O
A	O	C	C	X	J	S	S	Z	F	L	W	R	C	P
I	N	O	C	R	A	M	L	E	A	E	P	A	K	J
N	R	L	A	G	S	F	O	L	D	V	R	B	A	H
P	E	A	R	S	O	N	I	E	O	E	E	D	H	K
Z	Z	Z	U	L	H	E	E	L	V	R	C	P	S	T
Z	M	C	N	M	Y	E	G	M	A	Z	U	R	K	F
X	M	A	X	Z	I	C	L	T	E	H	U	M	E	I
Q	V	B	X	H	E	W	A	L	J	I	D	V	W	M
V	B	F	X	T	M	N	X	A	L	G	S	O	N	Y
A	N	Y	X	X	T	I	O	E	P	O	I	P	L	E

Top companies wordsearch – word list

BP
Barclays
Cocacola
Exxon
Ford
Generalmotors
Glaxo
Halifax
Lloyds
Marconi
Mercedes

Microsoft
Pearson
Rollsroyce
Shell
Siemens
Sony
Tesco
Unilever
Vodafone

Sales crossword 1

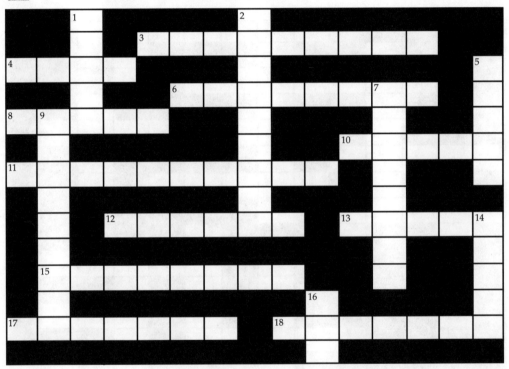

Across

3. Overcome this (9)
4. Let the customer ...
6. Potential customer
8. Not a good word to use
10. Do this with confidence
11. Energy and commitment
12. Don't talk, ...
13. Make enough of them
15. This should always be positive
17. Talked-up feature
18. Appealing fact

Down

1. Build this in
2. The art of haggling
5. Special?
7. The right temperature for the telephone
9. No weapons then
14. Connect with this
16. Don't forget it

Sales crossword 2

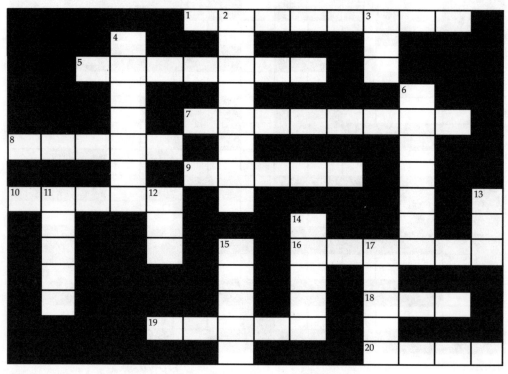

Across

1. Potential customer
5. Talked-up feature
7. Selling document
8. Nice to get a bit extra
9. Get these first and be clear about them
10. Ask about the budget
16. Don't talk, ...
18 ... and ye shall find
19. Build this in
20. Let the customer ...

Down

2. Personal lead
3. Subtle contact
4. Appealing fact
6. Getting on well
11. Special?
12. A word that's nice to hear
13. Don't forget it
14. Do with confidence
15. Make enough of these
17. Act and look

7

Problem-solving and planning

Purpose   These exercises allow participants to focus on challenges and problems and ways of solving them, or ways of improving current standards and methods.

Process   The exercises vary in their format and duration, although all require little preparation and can be used in a variety of ways.

Activities Boss for a day
Who killed the sale?
Cost-effective PR
SWOT analysis
Sales improvement brainstorm
Referral planning
The sales doctor
Persuasive writing skills 1
Persuasive writing skills 2
Preparing for a sales call

Boss for a day

Summary Working in small groups, participants identify the three key improvements they would make to their company's product or services, if they just had the power and the opportunity.

Objectives generating ideas/discussion
sharing viewpoints
self-analysis

Materials Flip chart

Timing 30–40 minutes

Procedure 1. Write the following trigger question on a flip chart and read it out to the group.

'If you were made Managing Director and you could change three things about one of your products/services, or the way they are sold or supported, what would they be?'

Ask the participants to write it down.
2. Divide participants into groups of 3–8 and ideally use different rooms. Ask the groups to discuss the question and then to summarize the main points and consider the consequences to them as salespeople.
3. After 20 minutes, reassemble the group and ask a spokesperson from each group who can present their main points. Allow time for a whole-group discussion.

Commentary This activity is a very good way of accessing and sharing the knowledge and expertise of the more experienced or successful members of the group with those who have less experience.

There is also a hidden benefit in that it also allows participants an opportunity to practise group communication and discussion skills.

Who killed the sale?

Summary   The sales equivalent of the post-match review that takes place with sports teams and their coaches. It is run as a 'whodunit'.

Objectives   focusing on improvements
analysis

Materials   Handout provided, flip chart

Timing   30–40 minutes

Procedure
1. Introduce the exercise as a sort of sales whodunit. Using their skills of detection and analysis, the participants will try to discover why a particular sale was lost, and what lessons can be learnt.
2. Distribute the handout and ask participants to work in small groups of 3–4, selecting one example each and working through the questions as thoroughly as possible. Explain that this should take about 20 minutes.

Distribute the handout and allow 15 minutes.

3. After 15 minutes, reassemble the group and ask each participant to review their examples and their conclusions, going through each of the four questions in turn. You can prompt discussion using the following questions, noting main points on a flip chart.

   ● How easy was it to analyse the sale in this way?
   ● What did you discover by doing this exercise?

Who killed the sale?

The purpose of this exercise is help identify areas for self-development and improvement. Take a moment to select a recent (or current) sale that you have lost (or are losing), or a particularly unsuccessful sales appointment/call.

Customer:

Brief details:

What reasons did the customer give for not going ahead with you?

What reasons do you believe, honestly, contributed to the call not being successful, or the customer not buying? List all factors you think apply, giving details and reasons where appropriate.

cont'd

If you could wave a magic wand and start the sale over again, what would you do differently (be as specific and as detailed as you can)?

What lessons can you learn from this sale that can help you in future sales?

Cost-effective PR

Summary   A group brainstorming exercise to identify imaginative yet practical ways of identifying good public relations opportunities at the local level.

Objectives generating ideas
communication skills

Materials   Handout provided, flip chart

Timing   45–50 minutes

Procedure   1. Introduce the exercise by asking participants the difference between trying to sell to a prospective customer who has heard of you or your company compared to a customer who has no prior knowledge or perception.
    Clearly it is easier if people have some preconception of an organization, so long as this is positive.
2. Explain that this exercise is designed to generate some practical ideas to increase the profile of you and/or your company in your target market and amongst your customers and prospects, in other words ways of generating low-cost PR.
    Although to reach the 'mass-market' via television and newspaper advertising and PR is very costly, on a local level and on an individual basis we can communicate to smaller groups of people much more effectively.
3. Divide participants into groups of 3–4 and distribute the handout provided. Ask participants to spend 10–15 minutes brainstorming, without any limits to their thinking, and then to put their ideas together during the following 10–15 minutes.

Distribute the handout and allow 20–30 minutes.

4. As participants are working on the problem, circulate between the different groups, stimulating discussion and perhaps dropping in a few ideas.

   The type of ideas that you are looking for are ways of effective personal marketing, such as writing articles for trade/local journals, giving presentations to industry groups and associations, becoming a member of such groups, running activities at local colleges and schools, and sponsoring or getting involved with charity events.

5. After 20–30 minutes, ask each group to present their ideas and recommendations to the rest of the group. Allow brief feedback and questions, making notes of the main points on the flipchart.

Cost-effective PR

The objective: to get your name/the company's name in front of as many local companies or prospects as possible, as cheaply as possible.

First brainstorm as many ways as you can that could achieve the above objective.

Next review your list, grading each idea on the following two categories:

- A, B, C for the quality of the idea (good (A), average (B), poor (C))
- 1, 2, 3 for the cost or difficulty in achieving it (1 = expensive, 2 = moderate, 3 = cheap)

Use this analysis to draw up a shortlist of recommended proposals and ideas, ones that you can implement and those that require wider involvement.

SWOT analysis

Summary   A version of the simple but highly effective technique for gaining a strategic and balanced perspective of a company or its products within the market place.

Objectives   strategic analysis

Materials   Handout provided, flip chart

Timing   30–40 minutes

Procedure
1. Ask if anybody has ever heard of a SWOT chart or SWOT analysis. Explain that it is a method used by marketing specialists and business planners to gain a strategic perspective of a company or product.

    Even if participants are familiar with the concept and have done a SWOT chart before, stress that it is valuable to do so regularly as things do change, including our judgements and perspectives.

2. Distribute the handout. Divide participants into groups of 2–3 and ask them to brainstorm and complete a list for each of the four headings the matrix for their organization or division, in relation to the market place and sales environment.

    (Alternatively you could focus the exercise on a particular product or product range.)

Distribute the handout and allow 20 minutes.

3. After 20 minutes reassemble the group as a whole and ask a spokesperson from each of the groups to present their lists of strengths, weaknesses, opportunities and threats. Develop any points that arise, and summarize these on a flip chart.

4. Ask the group how it would vary if it were completed by a

group of customers, rather than themselves, or by their competitors. Review the exercise with a general discussion, using the following questions.

- Quite often the same elements can be both strengths and weaknesses. Is this true for us, and if so, why is this?
- Are our weaknesses of our own creation?
- Of those listed and discussed so far, which do you believe is our single greatest strength?
- Of those listed and discussed so far, which do you believe is our single greatest weakness?
- Of those listed and discussed so far, which do you believe is our single greatest threat?
- Of those listed and discussed so far, which do you believe is our single greatest opportunity?

SWOT analysis

Strengths

> These are areas of excellence. They might include permanent features, or only temporary advantages. They might relate to technical features or quality, market-share or personal skills or key individuals.

Weaknesses

> These are the areas where an individual, a product or indeed company are the weakest.

Opportunities

> These are opportunities arising from the market-place or an internal source. For example, are you under-utilizing any strengths in your products or your people? Are there any changes taking place in the market that offer you a new set of opportunities?

Threats

> These may be internal (for example the imminent retirement of a key member of the sales team) or external (for example the appearance of a new and aggressive competitor).

cont'd

Strengths	Weaknesses
Opportunities	Threats

Sales improvement brainstorm

Summary   A useful brainstorming exercise which allows opinions and issues to be raised in a non-challenging and non-personal way, in order to involve salespeople in the process of business improvement planning.

Objectives   action planning

Materials   Handout provided, flip chart

Timing   60 minutes

Procedure
1. Introduce the exercise by asking if any participants have ever heard of the terms 'lateral thinking' or 'brainstorming'. After collecting definitions from the group, explain that they are thinking techniques made popular by a psychologist named Edward De Bono.
2. Optional (If the technique is new to the group or as a warm up exercise). Divide participants into two groups. Give one a wire coat-hanger, the other a paper-clip, glass ashtray or some other common object. Ask them to think of and write down as many uses as they can for each, no matter how outlandish the ideas may be. After 15 minutes see how many uses each group has generated. (Make sure they have included the main intended usage of each item!)
3. Write the trigger question on a flip chart. The question should be wide enough to allow for creativity and yet be specific enough to allow for a degree of constructive focus. An example would be: 'How can we increase sales by 10 per cent in the next 90 days?' Other topics could include: how to generate more leads and new prospects, overcoming discounting, making an impact in a sales call, differentiation, improving service, 'locking out' competitors, how to improve the product/service and how to make more calls in a month.

4. Divide the participants into groups of 4–8, ideally working in separate rooms.

5. Ask each group to agree a 'note taker' and a 'facilitator'. The task of the note taker is to write down **all** ideas and suggestions that arise, without judgement, no matter how ridiculous. The facilitator's job is to encourage as much participation and as many ideas as possible, **not** to judge or control the discussion, but to fan the flames of creativity.

6. Explain that each group should spend 25–30 minutes generating as many ideas as possible, and then a further 10–15 minutes to rank each idea and produce a shortlist of their best proposals.

7. After 40 minutes, reassemble the group and ask a spokesperson from each group to present their shortlist. Note the main points on a flip chart.

8. Ask participants to reform in their groups and distribute the handout, asking each participant to complete it for ONE of their ideas, also noting down their own or other people's ideas they think are of value or they would like to implement.

Distribute handouts and allow 5–10 minutes.

9. Finally, ask each participant to quickly review their list of actions. Remind them that good ideas and good intentions are not enough, only positive actions.

If brainstorming or lateral thinking is a new topic, there are a number of books available. In essence it involves 'sideways' thinking, assuming no constraints, and considering all options, regardless of how impractical or implausible they may first appear. 'In order to gain a high quality of ideas, it is first necessary to generate a high quantity of ideas.'

Sales brainstorming – action plan

Name:
Session:
Date:

The five best ideas arising from this session are:

1.

2.

3.

4.

5.

Key Actions:

1.

2.

3.

4.

5.

Reproduced from *Sales Training Games*, Graham Roberts-Phelps, Gower, Aldershot

Referral planning

Summary   A simple exercise to help provide salespeople with some practical ways of overcoming any obstacles they may experience in asking for referrals.

Objectives   confidence building
learning good practice

Materials   Handout provided, flip chart

Timing   45–50 minutes

Procedure   1.   Introduce the exercise by stating how effective referrals can be in gaining new leads and customers.
Referrals are one of the most cost-effective ways of increasing the growth of a business, yet go largely ignored by most salespeople. It costs several times more energy, money and time to generate a new lead or prospect than to gain a referral.
The majority of people will be pleased to give the names of colleagues who may find your products/services of value (assuming of course that you have done a good sales job as well). Indeed, nearly all of us at some time have recommended companies to friends or colleagues, such as garages, plumbers or travel agents. To highlight this use the following questions to prompt discussion.

● Who would rather spend two hours cold calling than contacting three customers for referred leads?
● Are referrals cheaper than other ways of generating new customers?
● Have you ever been asked for referrals by people who sold to you? Did you give them? If you haven't, would you give a referral if asked?

165

- Why do few salespeople tap the real potential of referrals? Do they think that people might say no? (Would it matter if they did?) Are they frightened of being too 'pushy'? Is it that they don't know how or when to ask for a referral? Do they forget to do so?

2. Explain that the first stage of removing these obstacles is to work out some effective questions that can be used to ask for a referral, and then to practise using them. Discuss an example of a suitable referral question, such as 'I know you're pleased with the work we did for you, and I was wondering if you could give me the names of two other fleet managers who might also find our services of value?'

3. Divide the participants into pairs and distribute the handout.

Distribute the handout and allow 20 minutes.

Circulate between the pairs to check that the questions are being developed and that where necessary participants are role playing possible questions.

4. After 20 minutes ask each pair in turn to present their questions and explain how they found the exercise to the group. Review the exercise with the whole group and note any points on a flip chart.

Referral planning

Write down some questions that you could use to ask for more referrals. Also consider when the best time might be to ask for these referrals.

Once you have a few questions, discuss or role-play them to make sure they are natural and easy to use.

1. _____
2. _____
3. _____
4. _____
5. _____

List the names of five customers you can approach for referrals using the above questions.

1. _____
2. _____
3. _____
4. _____
5. _____

Remember that the three keys to getting referrals are:

1. Ask – customers rarely give them without being asked, but never really mind when asked (providing you've done a good job and maintained a professional approach).
2. Ask for a specific number of referrals – usually two or three.

cont'd

3. Describe exactly what sort of person you would like as a referral, for example 'somebody who has the same sort of property' or 'another XXX manager within the organization'.

The sales doctor

Summary   Working in small groups, participants take it in turns to play the role of the 'sales doctor' to diagnose and solve key sales problems facing their colleagues.

Objectives   constructive discussion/problem solving
team-work

Materials   Handouts provided, flip chart

Timing   90 minutes

Procedure   1. Introduce the exercise by relating what happens when you go to the doctor. The doctor will first try to diagnose the condition before prescribing a cure. In this exercise participants will take on the role of the 'sales doctor', looking at ways of improving the business. (As the old saying goes, 'You don't have to be sick to get better'.)
2. Divide participants into groups of 2–3. Distribute the first handout (the problem), which asks participants to list three problems that could be related to a particular customer, a product, a marketing issue, or a skill element, such as dealing with price objections or closing.

Distribute the first handout and allow 10 minutes.

3. After 10 minutes you may either collect 'problems' and select one from each group to give it to another group, or simply allow the groups to select one of the three problems themselves. By selecting the problems for them, you can ensure a range of issues are covered and ensure and control the topics that will be worked on. As you give each group a 'problem', also distribute the second handout (the cure) for them to complete in the role of specialist sales/marketing

consultants. Participants will need 30 minutes for problem solving and 15 minutes to prepare their presentation.

Distribute the second handout and allow 45 minutes.

4. After 45 minutes, invite each group in turn to outline their problem and present their solution. The rest of the group can take on the role of the 'client', and at the end select which they thought was the best diagnosis and the best presentation. You may also consider allowing the group to ask a few questions at the end of each presentation.
5. After all the presentations have been completed, run a short discussion to summarize key points (which you can note on a flip chart) and close the exercise. The following questions could prompt discussion.

- Were you surprised by the quality of the solutions and ideas, given the short time allowed?
- Do you have more confidence in solving your own problems?
- How/when/by whom do you think the solutions can be implemented?
- What did you learn from this exercise?

Sales doctor (the problem)

Write down three current problems facing your sales activity or business.

These could be to do with a particular customer, a product, a marketing issue, or a skill element, such as dealing with price objections or closing.

One of these problems is then going to be passed over to a team of expert marketing consultants for expert diagnosis and recommendations as to potential solutions.

1.

2.

3.

Sales doctor (the cure)

You are a team of expert sales and marketing consultants, retained by the company to look into a particular sales/marketing problem and to arrive at an expert diagnosis and recommendations as to potential solutions.

Your proposed solution should be practical, and of course solve the problem, but there are no other constraints.

You will be required to give a short (10-minute) presentation explaining the approach and proposed solutions.

The rest of the group will take on the role of the 'client' and may ask questions at the end of your presentation.

Persuasive writing skills 1

Summary   Participants work with real samples of business writing to learn what makes for good (and bad) business writing.

Objectives   communication skills

Materials   Handout provided, at least 20 different business letters from around your office (if possible including competitors) – there should be examples of different content, style, format and spelling

Timing   30–45 minutes

Procedure   1.   Introduce the exercise by asking participants to consider how many letters the average customer may receive in the course of a month. (The answer may well be between 50 and 500.)

2.   Explain that this exercise is designed to increase awareness of written communications and what makes a letter, or any piece of written communication, distinct, readable and effective in achieving its objective, whatever that may be. Emphasize that an impression is always created by all written material, although that impression is not always a good one.

3.   Divide participants into groups of 2–3 and give a selection of your sample letters to each group. Distribute the handout and review the instructions.

Distribute the handout and allow 20–30 minutes.

4.   After 20–30 minutes, ask the groups to read out their sample letters and comment on them. Summarize the key points on a flip chart, and ask the group to make notes on them, and of course to put them into practice.

173

*This exercise is designed to be based on **real** examples taken from samples of business writing from around your own office and business. The reason for this is that the objective of good business writing (particularly marketing and sales) is not good English or correct grammar (although these are clearly important), but to generate impact, make an impression and prompt a positive reaction.*

Persuasive writing skills 1

Review the sample letters that you have and consider the following points.

- If these letters were all in your in-tray together, which ones would stand out?
- Are there any with spelling, typing or grammatical errors?
- Select the ones that you feel **best** achieve the writer's objective.
- Select the one that you feel **least** achieves the writer's objective (if he or she had one at all).
- Are there any letters, or parts of letters, that particularly impress you?
- Are there any letters, or parts of letters, that particularly fail to impress you?

Persuasive writing skills 2

Summary   Participants practise applying what they learnt in the previous exercise ('Persuasive writing skills 1') and develop sample letters.

Objectives   practising written communication

Materials   Handout provided

Timing   45–50 minutes

Procedure
1. Explain that this exercise is designed to help make written communication more distinct, readable and effective in achieving its objective, whatever that may be.
2. Divide the participants into groups of 2–3 and distribute the first handout (Persuasive writing skills 2A). (It might be best to allocate one type of letter to each group, thereby covering several examples in one session.)

Distribute the first handout and allow 20 minutes.

3. After 20 minutes, ask groups to read out their sample letters and briefly comment on them.
4. Distribute the second handout (Persuasive writing skills 2B) and ask groups to review and edit their letters, incorporating these ideas and the group comments.

Distribute the second handout and allow 15 minutes.

5. After 15 minutes, ask groups to read out their revised letters. Run a short discussion, based on the following questions.

    ●   What is it about the letters, or parts of the letters, that particularly impresses you?

- How does each letter stand out?
- How do the letters achieve their objectives?
- Do they conform to the AIDA model?

You could collect all the letters and then distribute a copy of each to all participants.

Persuasive writing skills 2A

Prepare **one** of the following letters.

- A short letter introducing yourself, the company or its products which will be sent out ahead of calling to gain an appointment.
- A letter following up a sales call to summarize why someone should buy from you and highlighting the unique benefits of the product/service in question (refer to a current item).
- A letter to follow up a less than successful sales call to thank them for their time, and to reinforce your USPs.

Persuasive writing skills 2B

The four elements of a good salesletter are:

A gain **attention**
I build **interest** (features)
D generate **desire** (benefits/value)
A prompt **action**

Remember to:

- Avoid jargon – use accessible language
- Make it easy to read – short sentences and neat paragraphs, the layout should be neat and easy to follow
- Don't write anything that you wouldn't say out loud
- Make sure there is nothing open to mis-understanding
- Check all spelling and grammar yourself, don't rely on a spell-checker on the computer; double check names and addresses
- Make it personal and sound friendly
- Use adjectives and descriptive language wherever possible
- Make sure it achieves your objectives

Preparing for a sales call

Summary   Participants develop their own 'presentation plan and sales kit' for future sales appointments.

Objectives   planning and organization

Materials   Flip chart

Timing   20–30 minutes

Procedure
1. Introduce the exercise by stating that normally you will have obtained information and created a positive impression by a previous phone call or written contact before any major sales appointment.
2. Ask participants what kind of preparation can be done before a sales call. Ensure the following areas are covered by your discussion and note key points on a flip chart.

    i.   Personal
- appearance
- focused attention
- no interruption

    ii.   Knowledge of the customer
- what is to be discussed
- previous meetings/contact
- any other information

    iii.   Environment (if in own office) or location
- planning
- punctuality
- preparation

    iv.   Materials (sales kit)
- note pad

- good quality pen (and a spare)
- literature
- samples
- order pad
- table-top presenter
- calculator
- business cards

In particular, stress the importance of the sales kit. Explain that in a recent survey, 20–30 per cent of all sales calls were incomplete because the salesperson did not have everything necessary to finish the call. This may include missing brochures, order forms, prices or simply a pen!

3. Divide participants into pairs and ask them to list **all** the items and materials that would be needed to complete a typical sales call to the highest possible standard and to the fullest extent (that is gaining an order).

4. After 15 minutes, reassemble the group and discuss each pair's list, noting any extra items on the flip chart. You can prompt discussion with the following questions.

- Why is good preparation important, if not vital?
- How is it of value to the customer?
- What are the benefits to you?
- What impression will readiness create?
- Is it true that clients buy people not products?

8

Role plays, practice sessions and case studies

Purpose Role plays or practice sessions are an essential part of any sales training course. These ready-made exercises are designed to add more variety to your training.

Process The exercises are similar in their format and duration and require some preparation. They can all use the role play observation sheet as a handout to prompt discussion from the observer's results.

Activities Appointment making
Thirty-second presentations
Chance encounter
Negotiation skills
Needs analysis
Think positive!
The big presentation
Telling is not selling
Presenting with power
Closing and trial closing

📄   # Role play observation sheet

Name:		

Skill	Check	Examples/Notes
Gained rapport		
Introduction		
Fact-finding questions		
Tested understanding		
Summarizing		
Empathy		
Stayed calm		
Controlled conversation		
Explained reasons		
Mentioned benefits		
Negatives		
Jargon/confused		
Attacking/defending		
Closing/shutting out		
Disagreeing		
Were objectives met?		
What worked well?		
What particularly impressed you?		
What could be improved?		
What did you learn or notice?		

Appointment making

Summary   A simple practice session around making sales appointments over the phone.

Objectives   confidence building

Materials   Handout provided, flip chart

Timing   60 minutes

Procedure   1.   Introduce the exercise to the group by asking 'How many people would like to be more effective in making appointments on the telephone?'
This can be defined as making fewer calls to get the same number of appointments or getting more appointments from the same number of prospecting calls.
2.   Divide the participants into groups of 3, with one person being the customer, the second the salesperson and the third an observer. Sit the customer and salesperson back to back so that no eye contact can be made. If available, use recording equipment and review during feed-back session.
3.   Distribute the handout and check groups understand the instructions.
Tell participants that the 'phone calls' are to last 5–10 minutes and be as realistic as possible.
If there is time, everyone in the group should play each of the three roles.
Ask observers to give adequate and detailed feedback on the good and bad points of each call.

Distribute the handout and allow 40–50 minutes.

4.   After 40–50 minutes, reassemble the group and lead a

discussion on what was learned, realized or reinforced. The following questions can be used to prompt discussion.

- How effective were the salespeople in gaining the customers' initial attention?
- What phrases and questions worked best?
- What particular phrases impressed you the most?
- What mistakes were made that are useful to learn from?
- Did the salespeople sell the 'appointment' or the product?

Summarize key points on a flip chart.

Appointment making

Salesperson's brief

You have been handed a lead from an exhibition enquiry, which due to poor handwriting has left some of the details a little vague. All you know is that you have to contact a Mr or Ms/Mrs/Miss (you don't know which) J. Huthwaite of K.L.W. Ltd. They are apparently quite interested, and your boss **expects** you to get an appointment!

Customer's brief

You have recently attended an exhibition, at which you collected several interesting catalogues and a few free key rings! As the Financial Director of a growing company, at any one time you are often looking at a range of different projects and tend to use exhibitions as a source of information on companies or products – in case you need them sometime in the future.

You do not take kindly to pushy salespeople who talk too much, but will be pleased to see anybody who can help you achieve your main goals of increasing the business and controlling costs, and who approaches you politely and professionally.

Observer's brief

Please observe (listen) to the telephone conversation and offer constructive feedback as to what happened, what worked and suggest (ask) what might have been improved.

Use the following points as a checklist:

- introduction and getting the conversation started
- use of questions
- overcoming objections
- talking versus listening
- asking for the appointment
- talking about the product/service versus the benefits of an appointment.

Thirty-second presentations

Summary   Participants develop and practise their own 30-second sales presentation.

Objectives   practising communication and presentation skills

Materials   Flip chart

Timing   20–30 minutes

Procedure   1.   Introduce the exercise by asking if anybody has ever read a book by Milo Frank entitled *How to get your point across in 30 seconds or less*.

In this book Milo Frank claims that 30 seconds is the optimum time to communicate with another person, and that you should practise condensing your message/s to this length and then repeating the phrases regularly throughout a conversation or presentation.

He also develops the theme along the lines of: 'If you can't express yourself, or your idea, in 30 seconds, you won't be able to do it in 30 minutes either.'

This '30-second' message is based on many studies of communication, and interestingly is exactly the length of most television commercials.

Run a short discussion around the following questions.

- Is it possible to condense any point into a 30-second message?
- If you can't express your idea in 30 seconds, you won't be able to do it in thirty minutes either. Do you agree with this statement?
- How long are most TV commercials?
- How long does it take to read the average newspaper advert or article?

2. Explain that with this concept in mind, this exercise will help you to develop a 30-second sales message (30 seconds is about 100 words of normal speech), that answers the question:

    'What do you do, how are you different and why should I buy from you?'

    Write this question on a flip chart and ask participants to work individually.
3. After 15 minutes, ask each participant in turn to read out their 30-second sales message.

If you are using video-recording equipment, it is best to let all participants give their presentation first, and then review all the presentations as a group afterwards.

You could have the best example typed and circulated and/or awarded a prize.

Chance encounter

Summary   A practice session with a difference. Participants get the chance to try to get the most out of a chance encounter with a busy managing director. It also highlights the need to be constantly prepared and always alert to new opportunities.

Objectives   communication
quick-thinking

Materials   Handout provided, flip chart

Timing   20–30 minutes

Procedure   1.   Divide the participants into groups of three and distribute the handout. Explain that one person will be the customer, one the salesperson and one the observer.

Distribute handout and allow 30 minutes.

2.   After 30 minutes, reassemble the main group and run a discussion around the following questions, making a note of key points that arise on a flip chart.

● How did the customers react to the salespeople?
● What could have been done differently?
● How can you be prepared for such opportunities?

This exercise can also be done in front of a group rather than in groups of three.

Chance encounter

Customer's brief

You are the Managing Director of a medium-sized company.

You are on your way to a meeting on the other side of the building and pass through reception to check for an important fax message for which you are waiting.

Whilst you are there a call comes through for you which you decide to take as you have a few minutes to spare.

You finish your call, and start to walk out of the reception and go on to your meeting. When you turn you are faced by the smiling face of an eager salesperson who is waiting in reception for another of your managers.

Salesperson's brief

You are waiting in the reception of a medium-sized company, and you are a little early for your appointment.

You notice a well-dressed man walk up to the receptionist and ask about a fax message. While he is there a call comes through for him, which he decides to take on the spot.

You overhear him give his name and title as Mark Johnson, Managing Director.

If handled correctly, this could be a unique opportunity for you to make a contact with the ultimate decision-maker and create a good impression.

As Mr Johnson puts down the receiver and ends his call, you walk over and …

Negotiation skills

Summary   A version of the classic negotiating skills game sometimes called 'Red/Blue', 'Prisoner's dilemma' or 'The Zulus and the Phalanx'. It allows participants to practise structured negotiation skills and identifies the communications dynamics that exist when two parties negotiate and highlights the need to focus on a 'win-win' solution, as a win-lose approach can often result in a lose-lose outcome.

Objectives   practising negotiation and communication skills

Materials   Handouts provided

Timing   60 minutes

Procedure   1. Divide the participants into two groups and distribute the first handout. Make sure participants fully understand how the activity runs.

Distribute the first handout.

2. Send the groups to separate rooms, so that they cannot be overheard. Ask each group to select a 'facilitator' and an 'observer'. The facilitator will help to structure and focus the group's discussion between rounds and be responsible for making final decisions as to the group's choice for each round. The observer's role is to complete the observation sheet whilst the exercise is in progress and to report back. They can still participate fully in their group's discussions.

Allow 5 minutes for the groups to assign roles.

Tell the facilitators that they have 10 minutes to discuss strategy and decide on which colour to vote on the first round.

3.   After 10 minutes visit each group, asking for their choice of colour for round one. **Do not** disclose this to either team until both colours are collected. Then inform each team of the other group's choice and their resulting score. Give each group the second handout so they can keep the score.

Distribute the second handout (score sheet).

Instruct the facilitators that they have 5–6 minutes to decide on their next choice. It is important to keep the time-pressure up.

4.   After 5–6 minutes go back to each group for their choice of colours, and continue the process. After rounds 4 and 8 offer the opportunity for a conference.
5.   Conclude the exercise by running a short group discussion around the following questions. Ask the observers to review their notes and making a note of key points that arise on a flip chart.

- How did the different personalities in each team interact and develop?
- How well did the facilitator guide the team?
- What happened?
- What did you learn: about yourself, others and negotiation?

In 90 per cent of cases, one or both teams read the instructions as 'getting the most points' not as it states 'positive' points, and therefore set about 'winning'. Participants who grasp this point are often overruled by the competitive and assertive nature of other team mates. As soon as one team realizes that they can't win, they often set about sabotaging the other team. The conference sessions often turn into an exercise in bluff, counter-bluff and deception.

Negotiation skills

Objective

The objective of this exercise is for your group to end up with an accumulation of net positive points based on the scoring system below.

Procedure

The trainer will visit your group and ask you to decide whether to play **red** or to play **blue**. He or she will not tell you the colour the other group has played.

When both groups have made their move, the trainer will announce the colours which have been played and these are scored as follows.

Group A plays	Group B plays	The score is	Group A	Group B
Red	Red	=	+3	+3
Red	Blue	=	-6	+6
Blue	Red	=	+6	-6
Blue	Blue	=	-3	-3

There will be **ten** rounds.

After the **fourth** round, the trainer will ask the groups whether they want to confer. This conference will only take place at the request of both groups. If one of the groups does not want to confer, then no meeting will take place.

After the **eighth** round there will be a second opportunity for a conference should both groups want one.

cont'd

The scores in the fourth and eighth rounds will be doubled and the scores in the ninth and tenth rounds will be multiplied by 3 and 5 respectively.

The objective of this exercise is for your group to end up with a positive score.

Negotiation skills – score sheet

	Colour played		Score	
	Group A	Group B	Group A	Group B
1st round				
2nd round				
3rd round				
4th round				

A conference may be arranged at this point if both groups request it.

5th round				
6th round				
7th round				
8th round				

A conference may be arranged at this point if both groups request it.

9th round				
10th round				

		Group A	Group B
	Total		

Reproduced from *Sales Training Games*, Graham Roberts-Phelps, Gower, Aldershot 197

Needs analysis

Summary   A chance for participants to practise and become aware of the dynamics at play during the first five minutes of a sales call.

Objectives   identifying customer needs

Materials   Handout provided, flip chart

Timing   60 minutes

Procedure
1. Divide the participants into groups of 2–3, with each participant filling the role of customer, salesperson and observer in turn.
2. Distribute the handout. Ask the 'customer' to complete the customer profile details. This will be the brief from which the customer and the salesperson will work.

Distribute the handout and allow 45 minutes.

3. After 45 minutes, re-assemble group and run a discussion based on the following questions.

    ● What worked well? Why do you think this was? What happened in particular (be specific)
    ● What impressed you?
    ● What do you think could be improved?

Role plays can be video-recorded or audio-recorded and then reviewed. You could also ask participants to draw up action plans while the main points from the exercise are still fresh in their minds.

Needs analysis

First, the 'customer' should complete the following 'customer profile' details for a contact that you know or for one of your current prospects/customers, including a likely objective for this call (such as to make an appointment, send literature, take sample, close a sale, research an account).

The customer and salesperson will both refer to this in the role play.

Company: _____
Type of business: _____
Main contact: _____
Position: _____

Role play a sales call with one person being the customer, one the sales person, and the other an observer.

After each 'call' or 'appointment' (of about 15–20 minutes), ask the observer to offer feedback or comments on what happened, and experiment with any suggestions.

Repeat so that every member of your group plays the customer at least once.

Think positive!

Summary This practice session highlights the need for salespeople to have positive beliefs in, and expectations of, every sales situation.

Objectives self-confidence
positive attitude

Materials Flip chart

Timing 40–50 minutes

Procedure 1. Introduce the exercise by asking participants if they have noticed themselves using positive self-talk in order to motivate themselves or others. For instance, we often tell ourselves to 'cheer-up' or 'not to worry'. In selling, our state of mind or attitude has a key part to play in the success or failure of each sales call. Introduce the following points as being a collection of comments by top salespeople on the importance of positive attitude.

- 'What someone is thinking has far greater influence than what they say. In other words, people can sense your 'attitude', by unconscious clues in your behaviour.'
- 'As a salesperson, it is vital to have positive beliefs and high expectations of every sales situation.'
- 'The sale is made in the mind of the salesperson, not the customer.'
- 'Whether you believe you can or whether you believe you can't, you're right!'
- 'In any meeting of two people, the person with the stronger mind set, or committed to the stronger attitude, will prevail.'

2. Review each statement, one at a time, and ask participants to think about and comment on what they think the statement means.

   It is not necessary to gain agreement on all of the statements at this stage – the second part of the exercise will demonstrate how each can be true. The main purpose of this discussion is to get participants **thinking** about the importance of positive expectations and how these can influence the customer.

   One example of positive expectations is trying to find a parking space – if we expect to find one, we invariably do, and vice versa. Another is that educational studies have also shown that the expectation of teachers of their pupils is one of the most important elements in the success and progress of that class.

3. Ask participants to vote on which they think to be of most importance, in influencing the positive outcome of a sales call what they say and do or what they are thinking?

   This may be the first time participants have heard such questions and they may find it a little strange, but be patient. The confusion is part of the process.

4. Divide the participants into pairs, with one person as the salesperson and the other as the customer.

   Ask them to role play the start of a sales appointment. The salesperson must act with the belief that this customer is not going to be interested and will be defensive, and that they will experience rejection. The customer should try to be neutral and simply respond to the salesperson as they would do normally.

5. After 5 minutes, ask the pairs to repeat the role play but for the participants to swap roles.

6. After 5 minutes, ask the salesperson to role play the start of the sales appointment with the customer, with the belief that they have **the best** product on the market for that particular customer and they are excited about telling all about it. The customer should try to be neutral and simply respond to the salesperson as they would do normally.

7. After 5 minutes, ask the pairs to repeat the role play but for the participants to swap roles.

8. After 5 minutes, run a whole-group discussion on the differences participants experienced. Be sure to draw attention to the things you noticed that happened when the different beliefs and expectations were adopted, stressing the importance of a positive attitude.

The following questions can help prompt discussion.

- How do your expectations influence others and the outcome of a sales call?
- How do the expectations of your customer influence your actions?
- How can you put yourself in a positive frame of mind?
- How easy was it to change beliefs and expectations?
- When you played the customer, what did the sales person **do** differently? Were there differences in eye contact, hand gestures, voice tone or body language?
- As a customer, which 'person' would you rather deal with?
- Which approach would be most likely to get the business?

Record any key points on a flip chart and conclude with the message that:

'You don't get what you deserve – you get what you expect! So think **positive**.'

The big presentation

Summary   A presentation planning and practice session that gives participants the chance to revolutionize their own sales presentation style.

Objectives   analysis
injecting dynamism into presentations

Materials   Handout provided, flip chart

Timing   60 minutes

Procedure   1. Introduce the exercise by describing it as being based on a real-life situation. Explain that it will help practise presentation skills and enable participants to understand better **how** and **why** they are different from their competitors.
2. Divide participants into pairs and distribute the handout. It is a good idea to read the handout aloud, adding emphasis to the story.

Distribute the handout.

3. Run a short discussion on how participants might approach the exercise, using the following points.

    ● Define your unique selling propositions (USPs).
    ● Understand how these can be related as customer benefits.
    ● Generate ideas as to what could be the format, not just the content, of the presentation, that is how it could be made unique, interesting and memorable.

4. Run the exercise, suggesting to the pairs that they allow 30

203

minutes for the development of the presentation and then 10 minutes to fine tune it.

5. After 40 minutes, ask each pair to give their presentation. Then offer constructive feedback (making notes of key points on a flip chart). At the end of all the presentations, ask the group to vote on the best one.

*This is a fun exercise, based on a true story. As an exercise it has a hidden purpose. Participants will get very involved in trying to design and deliver a dynamic presentation, which are important skills and a definite objective of the exercise. However, perhaps more importantly is that in the process they will examine **how** and **why** their products, services and company are different, and how they can make those unique selling propositions (USPs) stand out.*

The big presentation

You are waiting to a give a presentation to a very important prospective account.

Winning this account would make you **the** top salesperson in the company and contribute to about 30 per cent of your annual quota. However, there are five other main competitors also bidding, and this is the final presentation. Detailed proposals have been submitted and you have each been invited to give a short, final ten-minute presentation on the theme of 'Why we should do business with you'.

The presentations have been going on, one after the other, all afternoon, with a 30-minute gap after each one.

Yours is the final presentation.

You have been pacing up and down for the last two hours watching each one of your competitors go in and come out looking very confident. After talking to one or two of them, you realize that your presentation will simply be an echo of everything that everyone else has said. So, you decide that your only hope is to create something that makes you stand out and really differentiates you from everybody else, and make the panel of decision-makers put you to the top of the list.

However, you only have about 40 minutes in which to prepare your presentation, and it must not last more than ten minutes.

Telling is not selling

Summary   Participants practise selling with 'one arm behind their back' –
no questions or benefits are allowed in the exchange. The
activity highlights the effect on customers when features are
used more than benefits.

Objectives   communication skills

Materials   Flip chart

Timing   20–30 minutes

Procedure
1. Introduce the exercise by asking participants to discuss the
   difference between **features**, **benefits** and **you** appeal,
   making notes on a flip chart.

   - A feature describes what something is or does.
   - A benefit explains what value or advantage it will have
     for the customer.
   - 'You' appeal describes benefits made personal and
     specific to the customer's previously established needs,
     wants and preferences.

2. Divide the participants into groups of 3–4. Ask each group
   to select one of their actual products or services and to list at
   least ten features (only features) for this product/service.
3. After 5–10 minutes ask each group to list its features on the
   flip chart.
4. With either yourself or one of the more experienced
   participants playing the role of the customer, invite a
   volunteer from each group in turn to 'sell' its product or
   service to you, in front of the rest of the group.
   Each 'salesperson' must observe two rules:

- he or she is not allowed to ask questions,
- he or she can only refer to the list of features on the flip chart, in other words he or she cannot give any benefits.

Your response should be one of 'interesting, but so what?' If a salesperson is tempted to starting using questions or benefits, he or she is 'out' and another participant has to continue the sale.

5. When every group has attempted this very difficult task, run a short discussion to conclude the exercise, using the following questions.

    - How difficult is it to sell even the best product or service if we restrict ourselves to only features and do not ask questions?
    - What happens when we don't ask questions, and just present the 'product'?
    - Do customers automatically understand how the features relate to benefits?

Emphasize that many salespeople only present features and ask too few questions. The better your product or service (that is the more features it has), the more common this is.

Presenting with power

Summary   Working in small groups, participants identify the most important technical and emotional elements in selling their particular products or services.

Objectives   generating ideas/discussion
sharing viewpoints
self-analysis

Materials   Flip chart

Timing   40–50 minutes

Procedure   1. Write the following trigger question on a flip chart and read it out to the group.

'Considering both technical and emotional factors, what is most important to your customers or prospective customers and how do you best present this with regard to your product or services?'

Ask participants to write the question down. If they are unsure of the focus of the question, prompt them to start by considering features and benefits, how we present them, what aids we can use, and so forth.

2. Divide participants into groups of 4–8 and ideally use different rooms. Ask the groups to spend 20 minutes on discussion, and another 20 minutes to summarize the main points and consider the consequences of these to them as salespeople.

3. After 40 minutes reassemble the whole group and ask a spokesperson from each group to present their summary (each taking about 10 minutes, with whole-group discussion as appropriate).

This exercise is a very good way of accessing and sharing the knowledge, ideas and expertise of more experienced or successful salespeople in the group with the less experienced members.

Closing and trial closing

Summary   A practice session around the techniques of closing the sale, which highlights the dynamics involved in presenting a solution, product or proposal.

Objectives   confidence-building
communication skills

Materials   Handouts provided, flip chart

Timing   60 minutes

Procedure   1. Introduce the exercise by discussing key closing skills. You can use the first handout to prompt discussion.
2. Divide participants into groups of 2–3. Explain that one member of the group will play the role of the customer, one the salesperson and one the observer.
3. Distribute the second handout and ask the 'customer' to complete the customer profile and to give this to the salesperson and observer. Run the activity, asking participants to focus on three things:

- trial closing,
- overcoming objections, and
- gaining final commitment to proceed with the sale.

Ask the 'customer' to be as realistic as possible, neither too harsh nor generous in his or her reactions. The 'observer' should offer constructive feedback.
   If possible allow for each member of the group to play each of the roles.
4. After 20 minutes reassemble the main group and lead a discussion, using the following questions.

- What worked well? Why do you think this was? What happened in particular?
- What impressed you?
- What do you think could be improved?

Make a note of key points on a flip chart.

5. Distribute the third handout and ask participants to complete while the main points arising from this exercise are still fresh in their minds.

Role plays can be video-recorded, or audio-recorded and reviewed.

Closing and trial closing – key skills

- Most sales are closed by the customer buying by implied consent.
- We (as customers) are not good at making buying decisions, and have a tendency to procrastinate. That is why we need good closing questions.
- You may need to ask four or five (different) closing questions.
- Closing is about confidence – yours and the customer's – so always sound assured and assertive.
- You must create a sense of urgency – a reason to buy now.
- Make customers feel that their decision is right. Reassure them by giving the benefits and proof.
- Watch and listen for buying signals, these are the signposts on the way to a successful sale.

Closing and trial closing

In this activity, you will role play a sales call, with one person being the customer, one the salesperson and the other an observer.

First, the 'customer' should complete the customer profile below. Include a likely objective for this call (i.e. to close a specific size order). You will each use this to refer to during the role play.

Customer profile:

Company: _____
Type of business: _____
Main contact: _____
Position: _____
Objective: _____

Make notes or explain any other important information.

When you are the customer, base your approach on the customer profile and portray the situation as accurately as possible. Be sure to offer any realistic objections and questions, and see how the salesperson trial closes and gains final commitment.

The observer should feedback or comment on what happened, and you should experiment with any suggestions.

Run each 'appointment' for about 15 minutes. Repeat so that every member of your group plays the customer at least once.

📄 Closing and trial closing – action plan

Key skills/ideas	How I can use/apply them
1.	
2.	
3.	
4.	
5.	

9

Skill boosters

Purpose   This collection of trigger questions, tasks and ideas can be used during a sales course or a sales meeting to boost skills and attitude quickly and effectively. They can be used for discussion and to focus attention.

Process   Participants work individually or in small groups, making notes for a presentation to the whole-group when asked. Topics can then be reviewed and discussed during the meeting or session. It has been found that having genuine two-way discussion during sales meetings is one of the best ways of both motivating and training salespeople on a continuous basis.

Activities   Buying signals
Closing questions
Sales success formula: $E = MC^2$
Increasing order size
Follow up
Sales pipeline
Referrals
Time wasters
How to double your sales
Success definition
Goal setting
Lost sales opportunity
Best customers
Thirty-second presentation
Preparation
Sales skills
Sales analysis

Sales activity
Sales questions
Mental rehearsal

Buying signals

Take a few moments to complete the following tasks, making some notes.

1. Make a list of five possible buying signals.

    1. _____
    2. _____
    3. _____
    4. _____
    5. _____

2. Consider and write down how you know whether somebody is interested in buying.

    _____

    _____

    _____

    _____

3. Make a list of ten questions that could be used as trial or test closing questions to check for buying readiness.

    1. _____
    2. _____
    3. _____
    4. _____

cont'd

5. _____

6. _____

7. _____

8. _____

9. _____

10. _____

4. List behaviours to watch and listen for when looking for buying signals.

_____

_____

_____

_____

_____

Closing questions

Take a few moments to complete the following task, making some notes.

> Statistics show that we need to close, or ask for a buying commitment, at least five times if we are going to achieve above-average sales results. Most average salespeople ask for the order only once.

Write out, in full, five different types of closing question.

1. _____
2. _____
3. _____
4. _____
5. _____

Remember

You will need to regularly practise and revise your questions, if you want to improve your closing.

Sales success formula: $E = MC^2$

Take a few moments to complete the following task, making some notes.

> E = Enthusiasm
> M = Motivation
> C = Confidence

Discuss and list how you might improve:

- your visible level of enthusiasm and energy,
- your motivation level, and
- your level of confidence.

Also consider what reduces your enthusiasm, motivation and confidence.

Increasing order size

Take a few moments to complete the following tasks, making some notes.

1. List ways that you could increase the average size of an order or create the opportunity for repeat business.

    _____

    _____

    _____

    _____

    _____

2. What associated products or services might interest your customers and prospects?

    _____

    _____

    _____

    _____

    _____

3. What percentage of their total business do you have?
    _____ per cent
4. Set a goal of increasing your average order or account revenue by 20 per cent over the next three months.

Follow up

Complete the following tasks and note the response or effect of each.

1. Call every one of your ten most recent customers today and check that everything is going as promised and to their expectation.
2. Action any points arising.
3. Do something extra for these customers.
4. Send a 'thank you' card or letter to every positive contact.

Sales pipeline

Take a few moments to answer the following questions, making some notes.

1. What is your sales target for the next three months?

   _____

   _____

2. Based on current prospects and activity, what is your current expectation of exceeding this?

   _____

   _____

3. List ten things that you need to correct, improve or increase now to influence and strengthen your sales pipeline forecast for the next three months.

   1. _____
   2. _____
   3. _____
   4. _____
   5. _____
   6. _____
   7. _____
   8. _____
   9. _____
   10. _____

📑 Referrals

Take a few moments to complete the following tasks, making some notes.

1. Consider how you might go about asking for a referral from an existing customer or prospect. Write down the actual questions you might use.

   _____

   _____

   _____

   _____

   _____

2. Call or contact ten people this week and ask each one the prepared referral questions.
3. Write a short 'thank you' letter to all those that gave you a name, or passed your name on to others.

Time wasters

Take a few moments to complete the following tasks, making some notes.

1. Calculate how many hours per week you actually spend talking to customers or prospects.
   _____ hours per week
2. How could you increase the time spent talking to customers or prospects by 10 per cent?

   _____

   _____

   _____

   _____

3. List ten things that are non-essential sales activities that you currently do when you could be selling (in other words, sales-time wasters).

   1. _____
   2. _____
   3. _____
   4. _____
   5. _____
   6. _____
   7. _____

cont'd

8. _____

9. _____

10. _____

How to double your sales

Could you increase your sales by 100 per cent over the next 6–12 months? Could somebody else? Is it possible?

Often, the first hurdle you must face is your own self-limiting belief. If you don't believe something is possible, you find reasons (excuses) to provide you with proof. However, if you believe something might be possible you begin to look for opportunities to prove yourself right.

The only two things that you have complete control of, and therefore can vary in your sales approach are the **quantity** and **quality** of your sales calls. Put more simply, this means:

make more calls, and make each call more effective.

Calculate the effect of increasing your number of calls by 25 per cent per month and then your closing (conversion) ratio and/or order value by 25 per cent.

Neither of these goals is impossible, and yet when combined can lead to a virtual doubling of sales performance over a period of time.

Sales success = Sales skills x ATTITUDE x Sales activity

Follow this example, where a salesperson is making on average 16 calls per week, the average order value is £100 and the average conversion ratio is 4:1. This average salesperson's sales per week are £400.

cont'd

Reproduced from *Sales Training Games*, Graham Roberts-Phelps, Gower, Aldershot   227

Step 1	
Action:	20 per cent increase in call activity rate
Average calls per week: 16	increases to 20 calls per week
Average order value: £100	no change
Average conversion ratio: 4:1	no change
	Average sales per week: £500
Step 2	
Action:	20 per cent increase in order value
Average calls per week: 20	no change
Average order value: £100	increases to £120
Average conversion ratio: 4:1	no change
	Average sales per week: £600
Step 3	
Action:	20 per cent increase in conversion
Average calls per week: 20	no change
Average order value: £120	no change
Average conversion ratio: 4:1	increases to 1 sale per 3 calls
	New sales total: £799

The salesperson's new sales total is £799 per week.

Discuss and agree:

- Ways you could increase your conversion rate.
- Ways you could increase your call/appointment rate by 15–20 per cent over a six-month period
- Ways you could increase your average order/account/sales value over a six-month period.

Success definition

Take a few moments to consider the following questions, making some notes.

1. What does success mean to you?

    _____

    _____

    _____

    _____

    _____

2. How do you know when you are successful?

    _____

    _____

    _____

    _____

    _____

3. How will know when you are selling successfully?

    _____

    _____

    _____

    _____

    _____

Goal setting

Take a few moments to complete the following tasks, making some notes.

1. Write down **everything** that you would like to achieve in the next 12 months, including both personal and professional goals.

    Select ten of the most important goals, and put a deadline against each. Then identify one thing for each that you can do over the next seven days.

Goals:	Deadline	To do in next seven days
1.		
2.		
3.		
4.		
5.		
6.		
7.		
8.		
9.		
10.		

cont'd

2. Write down your sales goals for the next 12 months. Select ten of the most important goals, and put a deadline against each. Then identify one thing for each that you can do over the next seven days.

Goals:	Deadline	To do in next seven days
1.		
2.		
3.		
4.		
5.		
6.		
7.		
8.		
9.		
10.		

Lost sales opportunity

Take a few moments to complete the following tasks, making some notes.

1. Review your prospect list for the last six months and make a list of all the customers or prospects who either haven't bought yet or whose sales have declined.
2. Contact each by phone (first choice) or letter. Take time to re-qualify and listen.

You will be surprised how many opportunities you find if you put new life into your old sales leads and dormant accounts.

Best customers

Take a few moments to complete the following tasks, making some notes.

1. Applying the 80/20 rule, identify your top 20 per cent of prospects, accounts or customers, and list these clearly.
2. Draw up a schedule that allows you to contact each one every 90 days, with something new, interesting or different. (If you don't, your competitors will.)

Note: 80/20 means that 80 per cent of sales comes from 20 per cent of the customers or that 20 per cent of the products/services contribute to 80 per cent of the revenue.

The easiest and most profitable source of tomorrow's business is today's customers.

Thirty-second presentation

Take a few moments to complete the following tasks, making some notes.

1. Create and practise a 100 (approx.) word presentation that explains who you are, what you do, and why someone should buy from you.
2. Make sure it is exciting and benefit-oriented.
3. Use it at every opportunity, after all it will take less than a minute!

Preparation

Take a few moments to complete the following tasks, making some notes.

1. How well do you feel you prepare for each sales appointment?

   _____

2. List ideas for how could this be improved. (Aim to double your current level of preparedness.)

   _____

   _____

   _____

   _____

3. List any accessories, equipment and sales aids you could use, or use more effectively.

   _____

   _____

   _____

   _____

cont'd

4. Write down a complete list of your sales 'kit', and assemble it into an easy-to-use or accessible form.

_____

_____

_____

_____

_____

_____

_____

_____

Sales skills

1. Rate yourself on a scale of 1–10 for each of the following (with 1 being the least and 10 the maximum):

Preparation	1	2	3	4	5	6	7	8	9	10
Telephone skills	1	2	3	4	5	6	7	8	9	10
Prospecting	1	2	3	4	5	6	7	8	9	10
Rapport-building	1	2	3	4	5	6	7	8	9	10
Questioning	1	2	3	4	5	6	7	8	9	10
Active listening	1	2	3	4	5	6	7	8	9	10
Presentation	1	2	3	4	5	6	7	8	9	10
Objection handling	1	2	3	4	5	6	7	8	9	10
Closing	1	2	3	4	5	6	7	8	9	10
Problem-solving	1	2	3	4	5	6	7	8	9	10
Follow-up	1	2	3	4	5	6	7	8	9	10
Paperwork	1	2	3	4	5	6	7	8	9	10

2. Start with those skills that you scored lowest, and set about improving your sales skills by reading, training or coaching **on a daily basis.**

The only job security you have is to be more skilled tomorrow than you are today.

Sales analysis

Take a few moments to complete the following tasks, making some notes.

For each of the last three complete sales months or periods, calculate the following:

- Percentage over or under target
- Percentage over or under previous year's results
- Percentage of new customers
- Conversion ratio – number of total prospects divided by actual customers in each period
- Average order/account size
- Average number of calls per day
- Average sales per working day

Analyse this and, through careful thought and discussion, pinpoint strengths and weaknesses in your sales results or performance.

Sales activity

Take a few moments to consider the following tasks, making some notes.

1. How many calls or appointments do you make in an average week?

   _____

2. Set a clear goal of increasing your sales call activity rate by 20 per cent, starting immediately, **today**!
3. List all the ways that you can think of to achieve this, considering both removing obstacles and creating appointments or sales opportunities.

   _____

   _____

   _____

   _____

   _____

   _____

   _____

   _____

Sales questions

Take a few moments to complete the following task, making some notes.

Make a structured list of open questions that you can use and refer to during a sales call. They should move logically from establishing specific facts, identifying problems or needs, the implication of these, and ways of creating value in solving these. Also make sure they establish the boundary lines: money, the decision-making authority, buying influences, time-scales, buying criteria and competition.

_____

_____

_____

_____

_____

_____

_____

_____

_____

_____

_____

_____

_____

Mental rehearsal

Take a few moments to complete the following task, making some notes.

Identify a forthcoming important sales call or appointment.

Find a quiet moment to mentally rehearse everything about the event, seeing yourself performing superbly, and achieving a perfect outcome. Make the image as vivid, clear, colourful, large and real as you can. Live that moment in your mind, as if it were real. Associate it with the feeling of success.

10

Answers

2 Ice-breakers and energizers

Three-letter words

Persuasion: son, ion, era, sin, rap, sir, ran, pan, pin, pun, sip, sap, run, pus, rip, one, nap, nip, nor, use

Customers: sun, tom, cut, cot, come, rot, rut, store, crust, cross, cress, rust

Acronym quiz

IBM:	International Business Machines
SWOT:	Strengths, Weaknesses, Opportunities, Threats
TBA:	To be Advised
WYSIWYG:	What you see is what you get
E&OE:	Errors and omissions excepted
RAM:	Random Access Memory
VAT:	Value Added Tax
FOB:	Free on Board
USP:	Unique Selling Propositions
ROM:	Read Only Memory
FOC:	Free of Charge

Jargon quiz

Open question:	Requires a full answer; begins with who, when, where, what, why, etc.
Closed question:	Requires a 'yes', 'no', 'don't know'

	answer; begins with a verb, such as 'is it?' or 'can you?'
Test close:	A question that checks for commitment, such as 'does that sound good to you?'
Off the page offer:	Fill in the coupon, response-based marketing
Cold call:	Telephoning or visiting a complete stranger with no other previous communication
Referral:	A lead passed to you from a customer, friend or prospect
Cross sell:	Selling additional products to existing customers
S.P.I.F.:	Sales Person Incentive Fund
Net profit:	Gross profit less fixed overheads; what's left after everything has be accounted for (taken out)
Gross profit:	Sales price less the direct cost of a product or service
Buyer's remorse:	Regret in buying or making a decision
The 4 Ps:	Marketing term for the marketing mix of Product, Price, Promotion and Place
Customer churn:	The effect of customers switching suppliers to take advantage of better terms and prices

Euroland quiz

Austria:	Schilling
Belgium:	Franc
Bulgaria:	Lev
Cyprus:	Pound
Czech Republic:	Koruna
Denmark:	Krone
Finland:	Markka
France:	Franc
Germany:	Deutsche Mark
Greece:	Drachma
Hungary:	Forint
Iceland:	Krona
Italy:	Lira
Luxembourg:	Franc
Malta:	Pound
Monaco:	Franc
Netherlands:	Guilder
Norway:	Krone

Poland:	Zloty
Portugal:	Escudo
Romania:	Leu
Soviet Republic:	Rouble
Spain:	Peseta
Sweden:	Krona
Turkey:	Lira
UK:	Pound

5 Quizzes and questionnaires

Presentation skills

3. Both are important, but (b) would be more influential.
4. (f) – focus on your objective.

Rapport building

4. Firm handshake, eye contact, small talk, swap business cards, match or mirror the other person's mood or posture, discuss things you have in common, positive comments, stay calm and relaxed, smile, make a sincere compliment, use the customer's name.
5. People subconsciously make 'instant' judgements when they first meet someone.
8. (c).

Objection handling

1. True (usually).
2. Objections are telling you what you've missed and what's most important to the customer.
3. Selling is about convincing – not order taking.
4. Whilst not always true, it is a useful generalization.
5. Welcome and acknowledge – you can only answer stated objections. Also to remain calm and unflustered.
6. A condition is an immovable barrier to a sale, an objection, resistance.
7. One is specific, the other general.
8. You are selling (or closing) too early, without developing desire, need and value properly.
9. Lack of need, desire or urgency.

Prospecting

1. Consider all sources.
2. Fear of rejection, fear of failure; poor organization.
3. Recognizing the importance of persistence; keeping records to improve follow up; improving telephone skills; better targeting of customers; practise.
4. To avoid a 'feast or famine' effect.
5. As many as it takes!
6. Better targeting; follow up; handling objections; making more calls; time management.
7. This will vary, the ratio may be from ten prospects for every order or more.
8. As (6) above.
10. (a) or (b).
11. More sales; job security; better customers.
12. Define the 'ideal' prospect profile; set the goal for the number of new customers in three months; design the prospecting activity plan; write telephone script; make the calls; don't give up.

6 Group energizers

Sales jargon wordsearch

A	O	X	B	C	P	R	O	P	O	S	A	L	N	P
H	P	C	G	O	S	S	Y	C	B	C	Y	E	O	F
Y	M	P	Q	M	N	E	I	F	J	S	L	S	I	D
H	A	D	O	M	T	U	R	N	E	W	D	O	T	C
C	R	R	I	I	X	Y	S	U	C	C	K	E	S	E
T	G	E	W	S	N	E	G	O	T	I	A	T	E	E
I	I	F	T	S	C	T	X	I	I	A	R	J	U	N
P	N	F	C	I	J	O	M	B	O	J	E	R	Q	P
O	S	O	E	O	G	D	U	E	N	M	Y	F	T	A
A	F	C	P	N	L	M	P	N	N	A	U	T	V	Z
N	Q	A	S	K	E	D	P	T	T	T	B	F	C	P
H	T	V	O	Q	U	B	C	U	L	Y	B	D	N	H
E	U	F	R	H	P	Q	B	A	K	I	W	H	E	O
T	R	O	P	P	A	R	W	R	L	F	M	T	A	G
G	T	Y	R	E	F	E	R	R	A	L	X	N	S	Y

Top companies wordsearch

G	E	N	E	R	A	L	M	O	T	O	R	S	P	C
M	I	C	R	O	S	O	F	T	L	L	O	Y	D	S
E	E	O	Y	Q	Z	U	Z	K	E	U	M	A	I	K
Y	X	C	Q	O	C	S	E	T	N	N	I	L	I	Q
S	X	A	F	O	R	D	C	S	O	I	R	C	Y	O
A	O	C	C	X	J	S	S	Z	F	L	W	R	C	P
I	N	O	C	R	A	M	L	E	A	E	P	A	K	J
N	R	L	A	G	S	F	O	L	D	V	R	B	A	H
P	E	A	R	S	O	N	I	E	O	E	E	D	H	K
Z	Z	Z	U	L	H	E	E	L	V	R	C	P	S	T
Z	M	C	N	M	Y	E	G	M	A	Z	U	R	K	F
X	M	A	X	Z	I	C	L	T	E	H	U	M	E	I
Q	V	B	X	H	E	W	A	L	J	I	D	V	W	M
V	B	F	X	T	M	N	X	A	L	G	S	O	N	Y
A	N	Y	X	X	T	I	O	E	P	O	I	P	L	E

Sales crossword 1

		¹V						²N						
		A		³O	B	J	E	C	T	I	O	N		
⁴T	A	L	K					G						⁵O
		U			⁶P	R	O	S	P	E	⁷C	T		F
⁸C	⁹H	E	A	P				T			O			F
	A							I		¹⁰C	L	O	S	E
¹¹E	N	T	H	U	S	I	A	S	M		D			R
	D						T			C			
	S		¹²L	I	S	T	E	N		¹³C	A	L	L	¹⁴S
	H						E			L			M
¹⁵A	T	T	I	T	U	D	E			L			I
	K						¹⁶P					L
¹⁷B	E	N	E	F	I	T		¹⁸F	E	A	T	U	R	E
							N					

Sales crossword 2

						¹P	²R	O	S	P	³E	C	T	
			⁴F				E				Y			
		⁵B	E	N	E	F	I	T			E			
			A				E					⁶R		
			T		⁷P	R	O	P	O	S	A	L		
⁸B	O	N	U	S		R					P			
			R		⁹F	A	C	T	S		P			
¹⁰M	¹¹O	N	E	¹²Y	L					O		¹³P	
	F			E			¹⁴C			R		E	
	F		S	¹⁵C		¹⁶L	I	¹⁷S	T	E	N	
	E			A		O		M				
	R			L		S		¹⁸A	S	K		
		¹⁹V	A	L	U	E		R				
			S				²⁰T	A	L	K	

Further reading

Another excellent activity for a sales meeting or training session is to send participants a copy of one these sales books and ask them to give a short presentation to the whole group on the key points that they found of value and interest.

Here are some books that are suitable for this purpose.

Berry, M. (1998) *The New Integrated Direct Marketing*, Aldershot: Gower.
Blanchard, K. (1985) *The One Minute Sales Person*, London: Fontana.
Davidson, H. (1997) *Even More Offensive Marketing*, Aldershot: Gower.
Forsyth, P. (1992) *The Selling Edge*, London: Piatkus Ltd.
Girard, J. (1990) *How To Close Every Sale*, London: Piatkus Ltd.
Harvey, C. (1989) *Secrets of The World's Top Sales Performers*, London: Century Hutchinson.
Henzell-Thomas, N. (1990) *Sales Masterclass*, London: Hutchinson Business Books Limited.
Hopkins, T. (1983) *How To Master the Art of Selling*, London: Grafton.
Kennedy, G., Benson, J. and McMillan, J. (1980) *Managing Negotiations*, London: Hutchinson Business.
Laborde, G. Z. (1984) *Influencing with Integrity*, Palo Alto, CA: Syntony Publishing.
Miller, R. B. (1985) *Strategic Selling*, New York: William Morrow and Company, Inc.
Moine, D. J. and Lloyd, K. (1990) *Unlimited Selling Power*, Englewood Cliffs, NJ: Prentice-Hall, Inc.
Rackham, N. (1995) *SPIN®-Selling*, Aldershot: Gower.
Russell, D. N. (1996) *The Complete Guide to Quick and Easy Marketing that Works*, Aldershot: Gower.
Smith, D. W. (1996) *Managing Relationship Selling*, Aldershot: Gower.
Storey, R. (1997) *The Art of Persuasive Communication*, Aldershot: Gower.
Wilson, L. (1987) *Changing the Game*, New York: Simon & Schuster Inc.

90 Brain Teasers for Trainers

Graham Roberts-Phelps and Anne McDougall

The activities and exercises in this collection are designed to broaden perception, and improve learning, thinking and problem-solving skills. Using them is also a valuable way to boost energy levels at the beginning, middle or end of any training session.

The collection will help any group engage all five senses in their learning, and develop creative and lateral thinking, word usage, mental dexterity and cooperative team skills. Most of the activities require no more than a flip chart or OHP to run. And because they need only a few moments preparation, they can be planned into sessions in advance, or simply introduced to fill gaps, or to signal a change of direction, as appropriate.

Trainers, teachers and team leaders will find *Brain Teasers for Trainers* a rich source of simple, flexible, and easy-to-use exercises, as well as the inspiration for their own variants.

Gower

Gower Handbook of Training and Development

Third Edition

Edited by Anthony Landale

It is now crystal clear that, in today's ever-changing world, an organization's very survival depends upon how it supports its people to learn and keep on learning. Of course this new imperative has considerable implications for trainers who are now playing an increasingly critical role in supporting individuals, teams and business management. In this respect today's trainers may need to be more than excellent presenters; they are also likely to require a range of consultancy and coaching skills, to understand the place of technology in supporting learning and be able to align personal development values with business objectives.

This brand new edition of the *Gower Handbook of Training and Development* will be an invaluable aid for today's training professional as they face up to the organizational challenges presented to them. All 38 chapters in this edition are new and many of the contributors, whilst being best-selling authors or established industry figures, are appearing for the first time in this form. Edited by Anthony Landale, this *Handbook* builds on the foundations that previous editions have laid down whilst, at the same time, highlighting many of the very latest advances in the industry.

The *Handbook* is divided into five sections - learning organization, best practice, advanced techniques in training and development, the use of IT in learning, and evaluation issues.

Gower

Web-Based Training

Colin Steed

Web-based training is becoming one of the most important tools for trainers and courseware developers. The ability to deliver training and learning online to an individual's desk offers enormous flexibility for the organization as well as the employee, cost and time savings and the opportunity to keep pace with constant changes required for today's organizations to remain competitive.

Colin Steed explains how trainers can use self-paced, online learning to develop and train employees and improve their performance. He outlines the benefits and drawbacks of web-based training, looks at the cost considerations, and examines the elements that make up a programme. There is plenty of coverage of what is currently available on the market as well as in-depth case material drawn from organizations that have already begun to use the technology. Using step-by-step procedures, and assuming no technical knowledge, this practical and timely book will help you design you own web-based training strategy.

If you want to know what web-based training is all about and whether it's right for your organization, this book provides all the answers.

Gower